Shall We Dance

A Beginner's Guide to Ballroom Dancing

by

Eric Zimmerer

First Printing 2003
Shall We Dance: A Beginner's Guide to Ballroom Dancing
By Eric Zimmerer

Published by:

 Ace of Hearts Publishing
1154 West Olive Avenue Suite 116-B
Sunnyvale, CA 94086
www.DanceAce.com

Library of Congress Control Number: 2003090123

Zimmerer, Eric E.
Shall We Dance: A Beginner's Guide to Ballroom Dancing

ISBN 1-932358-09-9: $19.95 Softcover

Acknowledgement

This book is a collaborative effort. The author would like to thank the following people for their hard work, support and encouragement along the way: Yimin Wang, Edna Zimmerer, Robert W. Zimmerer, Robert N. Zimmerer, and Keiko Iwaisako. Without any one of them, this book would not have been possible.

Warning - Disclaimer

Contents

Intro

Why Dance?

There are so many reasons to dance: the joy of moving to music, meeting new people, exercise, romance... All these reasons are motivation to learn this new skill of dancing. What if it were easy? What if you could practice a few steps and then move out onto the dance floor with confidence? That is what this book is about. Teaching the absolute beginner how to lead or follow a partner through the most popular ballroom dances. This guide shows both the man's and the woman's steps, and explains what to do with your hands and arms as well. We break down the movements that make up a dance step and then put it all back together again with easy to follow foot print diagrams. Even if you start with two left feet you will be able to dance with confidence after reading a chapter. Dancing is an activity that is more and more fun the more you do it. Practice these steps in private, and you will feel good and look good in public.

This book is organized so the reader gains maximum benefit for the effort. Many dance books assume a great deal of knowledge about dancing, and a formal education in music. Some books even assume the reader knows how to dance already. This book makes no assumptions other than the reader is interested in Ballroom Dancing. The absolute beginner should be able to read through the text, look at the diagrams and start dancing immediately. You don't even need music or a partner to get started: just follow the foot prints and count the beats. Of course, dancing is a whole lot more fun with music and a partner!

Dancing is something that allows for endless improvement. At first it is satisfying to do the footwork correctly. After the footwork is memorized, the dancer can work on a relaxed and elegant dance frame. After that, a dancer may choose to construct a 'routine' out of the various steps, and add new steps to their repertoire. Accomplished dancers and absolute beginners all improve over time. Don't expect to be perfect the first time you step out onto the dance floor, but this book will teach you how to be confident in your ability and help you enjoy your journey to becoming a great dancer. The first and most important step is to have fun!

A Dance is a Dance: Categories

Ballroom dances fall into three main categories: smooth dances, rhythm dances, and Latin dances. Each category contains many individual dances which share similar characteristics that share the same look and feel relative to the other categories. Individual dances in each category overlap significantly in technique so that learning one dance makes it easier to learn the others. There is significant borrowing of step patterns, leading techniques, movement, and styling among the dances.

Smooth Dances

The smooth dances are the Waltz, Foxtrot, and Tango. What makes a smooth dance? It is the way the dancers seem to float on air as they glide across the floor. The continuous graceful movement of the dancers mirrors the flow of the music. Smooth dances exemplify the grace and balance of deliberate, controlled movements. Smooth dances, as a result look elegant, sophisticated, and refined. Smooth dances may be slow or fast depending on the tempo of the music, but the attitude of the dance is graceful.

Rhythm Dances

The rhythm dances are not concerned with looking elegant and sophisticated, they are all about dancing to the beat. Rhythm dances generally employ faster music with a stronger beat than the smooth dances. It is possible to rhythm dance to slower songs, but why walk when you can run? The most famous rhythm dances are the East-Coast Swing and the West-Coast Swing. Swing dances have many names and nuances such as the Jitterbug, the Lindy Hop, the Hustle and Jive dancing. Some people consider the Nightclub 2-Step to be a rhythm dance, some consider it to be a smooth dance. It has elements of both and can fit in either category depending on who is dancing and how fast the music is.

Latin Dances

The Latin dances emphasize style, and accentuate the beat with dramatic movements and flourishes. Latin dances have a distinctive style that includes sharp movements, 'Cuban' hip motion, and dramatic poses. Latin dances also have a shared ancestry in that they originated in Latin countries. The Rumba, Cha-cha, and Salsa are all Latin dances.

Spot Dance vs. Traveling Dance

Some dances take place more or less in the same place. These are called 'Spot' dances because the couple stays in one spot. The Rumba, Cha-cha and Swing for example, are all spot dances. The couple makes use of one small area of the ballroom, adapting their dance to the music and the space that is available around them. Other dances, such as the Tango, Waltz and Foxtrot are traveling dances where the couples move around the ballroom according to the Line of Dance. (see below) Even the Spot dances allow the couples to move around a bit to take advantage of open space, closer or farther from the loud speakers, more or less lighting, etc. Some couples move faster than others, some move slower, but all dancers share the responsibility to avoid collisions. Each dancer will be looking over their partner's shoulder to make sure there is space to perform a pattern or to warn of possible collisions. If the dance floor is crowded, the leader must use his judgment to fit his patterns to the space available. It is better not to attempt a large pattern if there are too many dancers in the space already.

Line Of Dance

There are very few rules that a beginner needs to be aware of in ballroom dancing. The Line Of Dance is one of those rules. What would it be like driving on a freeway without lanes? Without the convention of driving on the right hand side of the road? Line of Dance is the convention that prevents head-on collisions in traveling dances. To follow the Line of Dance, think of the ballroom as a race track oval with traffic flowing counter-clockwise. As far as lanes go, the outside lane closest to the edge of the dance floor is the 'fast lane', and couples dance progressively slower the closer they are to the center of the dance floor.

Style

Style sets each dance apart from the others. As an example, the careful student will notice that there is a 'box' step in the Waltz, the Foxtrot, and the Rumba that are essentially the same from the standpoint of where to put your feet. But *how* you put your feet, what your upper body is doing, and how your body reflects the music are very different in each dance. Watching good dancers is a tremendous aid in learning style. Some teachers emphasize style from the very beginning, others wait until the basic patterns have been memorized before adding 'style'.

Without the style element, the dances lose much of their personality. Yes, the Waltz has three beats, but the rise and fall is significant too. The Foxtrot and the Rumba both have four beats, but the brisk, walking style of the Foxtrot is a stark contrast to the slow, sensual Rumba. Competition dancers focus a great deal of energy on their style. This is one of the elements that sets the great dancers above the rest. (Competition dancers frequently have a 'routine' that both dancers follow, so there is no leading or following: each step is planned and performed according to a script. Some of these dancers are quite good at leading and following, yet others only look good with their competition partner) For a beginner, style is less of a concern.

Beginners are occupied with memorizing the patterns and developing their leading/following skills. Once the dancer is comfortable leading or following a variety of partners on the dance floor, then it is time to focus on style. Smooth dances require good posture and calm body language, like the waltz. Latin dance styling exaggerates the hip movements and makes use of dramatic hand movements. You will notice many dance studios and ballrooms have an abundance of mirrors. These mirrors are very useful in refining one's style. If a motion feels right, look in the mirror to see how it looks. More (or perhaps less) 'style' may suit any particular move. In the end, style is personal, and entirely up to the individual's taste. Breaking conventions can even be a style. Each ballroom crowd has a 'norm' for style. Watch what the other dancers are doing and try to fit in by incorporating just a little bit of what the crowd is doing.

Dance Frame

One of the most important fundamentals of Ballroom dance is what is known as the 'Dance Frame.' The Dance Frame is a dancing term for the posture and relative position two dancers maintain for a dance. The most essential dance posture and relative position for ballroom dancing beginners is called the Closed Dance Frame. This term describes the way two dancers stand facing each other with their arms and hands in contact. With a solid frame, dancers look elegant and stylish. Leading and following are greatly enhanced by a solid frame.

What does a dancer have to do to maintain a solid Dance Frame? The basic elements of a solid dance frame are:

1) Partners face each other with shoulders parallel.

2) The man places his right hand on the woman's left shoulder blade with his fingertips touching the middle of her back.

3) The man's right arm is firm, with the elbow up and away from his side.

4) The woman places her left arm on top of the man's right arm, with her left hand on his upper arm just where it meets his shoulder. The woman should hold her left arm firm so she can respond to her partner's forward movement. If her arm is limp, she may get stepped on as a result. In this case, it is actually the woman's error that causes her to be stepped on!

5) The woman makes a V with her thumb and fingers so that she can feel side to side movements as well as forward and backward movements of her partner.

Closed Dance Frame

6) The man's left hand is held out with the palm open and perpendicular to the floor. The left elbow is up and away from his side.

7) The woman places her right hand in, and slightly on top of, the man's left hand. Her elbow is up and away from her side also.

8) Both the leader and the follower keep both their arms firm. This firmness is what allows the communication of forward, backward, side to side, etc. If either person's arms are not firm, the arms wiggle or flap and the dancer's collide, step on each other, or any number of ungraceful things can happen.

9) Offset by two inches. This one is critical! What 'offset' means is that the leader should hold the follower slightly to his

Closed Dance Frame

right and look over her right shoulder. The follower should be sure to stand slightly to the left of her partner while keeping her shoulders parallel to her partner's shoulders. This offset allows the dancers to take a step forward without knocking knees or stepping on feet. (We will cover stepping on feet more thoroughly later) If the dancers line up 'nose to nose and toes to toes' and take a step, they will knock knees. The dancers should line up nose to nose, toes to toes and THEN EACH DANCER MOVES TWO INCHES TO THEIR LEFT. This offsets the dancers so they may take a step directly forward without landing on their partner's foot.

What if you are left handed? Left handed people dance exactly the same as right handed. There is no 'right handed grip' or 'left handed grip' in ballroom dancing. People all dance the same.

To review the Closed Dance Frame: The man has his right hand on the woman's left shoulder blade, both his elbows are up and his left hand is at a comfortable height for his partner to place her hand in his. The woman has her left hand in a V on top of the man's right arm with her hand on his upper arm just below the shoulder. She has her right hand in the man's left hand with both of her elbows up and the dancers are offset so they may each take a step forward without knocking their partner's knees.

In the Latin dances (Rumba, Cha-cha, and Salsa) the dance frame is a Closed Dance Frame just as above with the exception that the man's left elbow is not up and out to the side but rather it is held out in front of the man so that the dancer's hands and forearms are vertical, and are in contact. This makes for a tighter dance frame and allows the dancers to stand closer together.

As you may have guessed, there are many kinds of dance frames and positions which depend on the dance, the step and what the leader chooses to do. The most important position in Ballroom Dancing for the beginner is the Closed Dance Frame. The second most important position is the Open Dance Frame. The Open Dance Frame is when the man and woman face each other but stand a bit farther away from each other holding hands. (Holding just one hand is called the Half Open Dance Frame) In the open position the man holds the woman's right hand in his left hand. As in the Closed Dance Frame, it is important to maintain good posture in the Open Dance Frame.

Communication

Dancing is interactive, so it is a good idea to tailor your dancing to your partner. Starting small is always a good idea for the leader. Get used to your partner with simple patterns and let her get used to your leading, too. While expert dancers can really impress beginners with all the moves they know, it may not be much fun for your partner to stand next to you while you show

Latin Dance Frame

off. It may seem impossible at the start, but eventually it will be easy to have a conversation while dancing. Some people prefer to enjoy the music and the 'nonverbal' communication. Be sensitive to this as well.

Leading

In ballroom dance there is a leader and a follower for each couple. Convention has it that the man leads and the woman follows. For the men, this means they get to decide which steps to

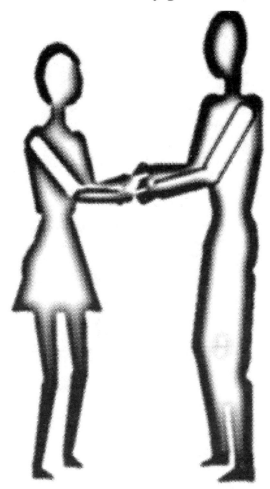

Open Dance Frame

do and in what order. The leader gets to choose the steps and express them to the music and the mood. With privilege comes responsibility! The leader is responsible for communicating the steps to his partner. A solid dance frame is the best (only?) way to communicate where the next steps will be going, and what the follower should do next. Confidence helps to firm up the dance frame and lead with strong signals. In general, raising the woman's right hand indicates a turn. The direction the leader wants the follower to turn is determined by the direction the hand goes. The leader will often use his right hand to gently pull the lady forward to maintain the dance frame while taking

Half Open Dance Frame

backward steps, or let go with the right hand to indicate the couple is separating from closed to open dance frame. For beginning followers, it often helps to use the right hand to guide the lady through under arm turns. Leaders should be sensitive but firm.

Tip: Let your dance partner determine the level of your dancing. For example, when dancing with someone more experienced than yourself, try all your complicated patterns. Your dance partner may well give you some helpful advice, or at least will help you to practice your form. When dancing with a less experienced partner, select less complicated patterns and send clear leading signals to encourage your partner.

Following

A good follower does not anticipate the next step, but is prepared to respond to whatever the leader does. This is greatly facilitated by a good dance frame and a positive attitude. Feel the motions, respond to the forward, backward, side to side movements and be feather-light in the arms of your partner.

One of the joys of dancing is to float around the room with your partner as a single unit. The difference between floating and floundering can be made by a good follower. Conventional wisdom says that men take three times longer to learn ballroom dancing than women. Leading the steps is one of the reasons it takes men so long. While they are performing the current motions, they must be planning the next step, the next pattern, watching for and avoiding collisions, and giving proper signals to their partner about what will happen next. Many beginning dancers are overwhelmed by all this. If your partner is having difficulty, 'helping' him with his steps and instructing him in how to lead will probably confuse him even more. The best thing for a follower to do is follow enthusiastically and compliment successful dancing. Nothing succeeds like success, and building your partner's confidence will help him help you to enjoy the dance.

Starting out right: finding the beat

It is a common complaint among beginners that finding the beat is difficult. Yes, it can be difficult at first. But the good news is that it gets easier and easier over time. The first thing to listen for is the types of ballroom dance music. Ballroom dance music may be constructively broken down into two categories: 1) Waltz, and 2) Everything Else. This makes for a simple first test: Is it a Waltz?

Waltz music is the easiest music to identify because the music counts one-two-three one-two-three with the emphasis on the first beat. If it is a waltz, you know what to do: dance the waltz! If it is not, you have more questions to answer. If it is a fast beat, you may have a Foxtrot or a swing on your hands. If you hear Frank Sinatra singing, chances are it is a fox-trot. If it has a strong beat that makes you want to jump around, it is perfect for the swing. If it is a slower beat, you may have a rumba or a two step. Night Club Two Step music is in 4/4 time without a 'Latin' sound to it. If the music has a 'Latin' sound and it is slow, it is most likely a Rumba. Fast Latin music is suitable for Salsa and Cha-cha.

The Tango has a distinctive beat: slow slow quick quick slow. It is the most dramatic music because of this signature beat. Tango music can be slow or moderately fast. Listen for the dramatic beats and watch the dancers pressed against each other for confirmation of a Tango. It is very likely that the ballroom DJ will announce before-hand what type of dance is next. This makes it really easy: do what the DJ says.

Foxtrot, Swing, Rumba, Cha-cha and Salsa music is written in 4/4 time. That means there are four beats per measure. There are a great number of dances that are set to 4/4 time, so it is possible to dance your favorite 4/4 dance to any 4/4 music. That means it is possible, and fun, to dance a Rumba to a slower Cha-cha, or to dance a Cha-cha to a slower Salsa tune. It is also possible to dance the Foxtrot to a slow Swing tune, or to dance the Swing to a fast Foxtrot because they are all in 4/4 time. It is NOT possible to dance a Waltz to anything other than a Waltz.

Once you have determined the style of dance, count the beat to yourself as you take the floor with your partner. When you are both ready, in the proper dance frame, it is up to the man to take the first step. As a beginner, don't wait too long to take the first step; it is bet-ter to plunge in and make corrections than to wait for the perfect start.

Smooth start

When the music is playing, and the couple have assumed the appropriate dance frame for the dance style and music, it is good to start smoothly, and on the proper beat. Generally speaking, it is better to start with the basic step of the dance than to start with a more complicated pattern that throws either partner into motion too suddenly. A gentle start is preferable, leaning into the fist step with small steps to get started.

TIP: For leaders, it is easy to surprise a new partner with unexpected moves. It is better to lead the lady a little too early than too late until she is familiar with your leading.

TIP: For followers, it is said that a woman can do anything she wants so long as she does not lead. Some people find that closing their eyes makes it easier to follow.

Information Overload

The novice leader is often overwhelmed by the many elements that must be taken into consideration: Dance Frame, proper steps to dance patterns, leading his partner, following line of dance, avoiding collisions, and steering a course among the other dancers. The beat of the music sometimes gets lost in among these considerations. It is very common for women to notice that their partner is not on the beat. The best option is to ignore it. If a dancer is overwhelmed by the other considerations, reminding him that he is not on the beat will only make things more difficult for him. If the man finds the beat, great, if not, thank him for the dance when it is over and seek another partner if you wish.

Keeping the beat

In many ways, dancing is like walking to music, so don't worry about getting every step just right. If you make a mistake, keep walking to the music and chances are people will not notice! One of the easy things about the basic Waltz steps is that the dancers take one step for each beat of the music. How can anything be simpler? When you hear the beat, take a step. Alternate between stepping with your right and left foot (do not hop on one foot!) and you are dancing the Waltz! Listen to the music, step in time with the music, and enjoy the dance. If you lose the beat, don't worry, dance halls do not have spot lights on the beginning dancers, and a beginner can dance without fear of being observed by everyone in the room.

Some people (men and women) are rhythmically challenged. For most people it is a temporary problem caused by trying to coordinate one's feet, arms, hands, body, and partner all at the same time. Rhythmically challenged people quickly master the steps and dance to the beat if they work at it. If your partner happens to be dancing off the beat, think about how you would like to be told such news. As a beginner, it is easy to be making progress on all the other things and discover that the beat has gotten away from you. Some people can adjust their steps and 'catch up', others do better by stopping and starting again the next time the beat comes around.

If your partner is consistently missing the beat, relax and go with it, make the best of the situation and your partner may relax and find the beat. If not, you can always decline the next dance. If a woman is not dancing to the beat, and her partner is, she is not following well. Try leading a simple pattern to let her get used to dancing on the beat and following the leader. The woman must react to what the man does, and it helps to have a relaxed attitude and not make assumptions about what pattern he will lead next. Relax and go with the music!

Ballroom Dance Etiquette

Basic Ballroom Etiquette is so simple... Just follow the golden rule: do unto others as you would have them do unto you. Always be polite and courteous. Show enthusiasm, and always thank your partner for each dance.

For Men: If you want to dance with a specific woman, ask nicely and do not take a negative response personally. Ask with the expectation that the answer will be 'yes'. If a woman refuses your request repeatedly (more than twice) cut your losses and move on to another dancer. Keep this in mind when you refuse to dance with someone a second or third time; most people will not ask again.

For Women: Body language will tell the experienced dancers that you are interested in dancing. Eye contact also indicates a desire to dance. Making eye contact with someone increases the chances that that person will ask you to dance. It is more and more common for women to ask a man to dance, so if you see a man you would like to dance with, don't wait, go ask him!

Right of Way

When dancing it is every dancer's responsibility to avoid collisions. However, collisions are still too common on the dance floor. When preparing for a pattern, the leader must be aware of how much space the pattern requires, and compare that to the space available on the dance floor. If there is not enough space, DON'T LEAD THAT PATTERN!

Many optimistic leaders gamble on the odds that enough space will open up by the time the couple gets there. This is one reason why collisions happen. When a collision does occur, apologize immediately, even if it was not your fault. Your partner will think better of you, and so will the partner of the person who crashed into you.

Conventions used in this book

Foot print diagrams are shown from the dancer's perspective. If a dancer were to look down at their own feet and map out where the dance steps go, that is what the foot print diagrams show. In most cases, the man's or woman's foot prints are shown separately so the man or woman can focus on what their own feet should be doing.

Man's & Woman's footprints

The dark foot prints are fully weighted steps, showing a step with a change of weight.

Light foot prints are unweighted steps, which can be either a starting point where the foot bears no weight, or a step where the dancer does not transfer weight to the foot.

Dark & light footprints: weight on ball of foot

The dark & light foot prints illustrate a step where only the ball of the foot touches the floor. The heel should not touch the floor on this step.

To illustrate dance steps, or patterns, it is necessary to have a starting point. The starting point is shown as a weighted foot and an unweighted foot together. The man always starts a pattern with his weight on his right foot and his left foot free.

In the example above, the man starts with his feet together and his weight on his right foot. The right foot is dark and the left foot is light to show which one has the weight and

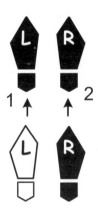

which one is free to take a step. The example shows the man taking a step forward with his left foot first (the arrow with the number 1 shows the man taking a step with his left foot and placing his weight on it) and then a step forward with his right foot (the arrow with the number 2). At the end of the example, the man will be standing with his weight on his right foot. There are certain fundamentals of dance which make the whole exercise a little simpler: the dancer's weight shifts from foot to foot most of the time. In many instances, dancing is very much like walking to the music.

Dancing Steps

There are many dance schools and many ways to describe how to take a dance step. There are also many names for these steps. The following list is a partial list of the step names that are useful to know when learning ballroom dance. The names are the ones that the author is familiar with, having heard the names and the definitions on several occasions from several dance schools.

Walking Step: This is a very simple step taken so that the heel touches the floor first and then the toe touches down.

Heel-Toe: A step taken so the heel lands first and then the weight is rolled onto the ball of the foot. Same as the walking step.

Toe-Heel: This step has the dancer's foot touching the toe to the floor first and then the heel.

Side Step: As the name implies, this is a step taken to the side. The dancer's weight lands on the ball of the foot unless otherwise stated.

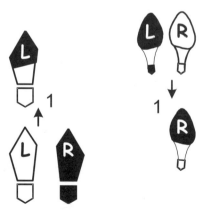

Rock Step: This is a step forward, backward, or to the side where the stepping foot touches just the ball of the foot to the floor and specifically does not let the heel touch the floor. The weight of the dancer shifts to the stepping foot momentarily. After the rock step, the dancer takes a rock-replace step. The illustration above shows the man standing with his weight on his right foot as he takes a rock step forward onto his left foot, the woman standing with her weight on her left foot as she takes a rock step back onto her right foot.

Rock Replace: This is a step which follows after a rock step. If a dancer takes a rock step with the left foot, the rock-replace step puts the dancer's weight onto the right foot. If a dancer takes a rock step with the right foot, the rock-replace step puts the dancer's weight onto the left foot.

Fifth-Position Step: This is a ballet dance term that indicates the feet are perpendicular to each other. If the right foot is facing forward, then the left foot will be facing the dancer's left, pointing perpendicular to forward. at a 90 degree angle from the right foot. There are several dance patterns which take their names from this distinctive positioning of the dancer's feet.

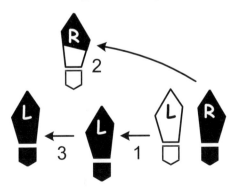

Buzz Step: This step has the dancer's feet crossing in front of each other (step 2) or in back of each other as the dancer steps sideways. The dancer will be facing perpendicular to the direction they are traveling in.

Touch Step: This is a step where only the toe of the stepping foot touches the floor and there is no change of weight. That is to say, if the dancer is standing on the right foot and does a touch step with the left, the dancer's weight will remain on the right foot throughout the step.

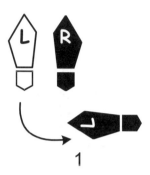

Hook Step: This is a step to help a dancer to turn or prepare for a turn. The hooking foot steps around and behind the standing foot.

Dancing is a physical activity. You can read all you want but you won't get good at it until you get out of your chair and dance! Learning the patterns in this book is a great start. You will find however that 'putting it all together is where the magic happens. Knowing lots of patterns does not make a dancer great; emotional content and style are what make a dancer great!

* * *

Waltz

The Waltz is the oldest ballroom dance and the most famous. The Waltz is elegant, graceful and easy to learn. The Waltz is a smooth dance, and has a distinctive rise and fall motion that sets it apart from all other dances. Waltz music is easy to recognize because of the 3/4 time. The first question to ask when hearing dance music is: 'Is this a Waltz?' Waltz music has three beats per measure counted 1 2 3 1 2 3 1 2 3 ... The accent is on the one, and each beat indicates a step the dancers will take.

The Box Step

The basic pattern of the waltz is the box step. This is one of the most popular steps and is 'borrowed' by many other dances and adapted to make it fit in with the various styles and rhythms. Dancers begin the Waltz box step in the closed position. The closed position is the same as the closed Dance Frame from the previous chapter. On the first beat, the man takes a step forward with his left foot while the lady takes a step back with her right foot. On the second beat the man takes a side step forward and to the right with his right foot, the lady takes a side step with her left foot. On the third beat the man takes a step with his left foot to bring his feet back together and the lady takes a step with her right foot. Note that both dancers change their weight so that the man has his right foot free for the next step and the lady has her left foot free (no weight on the foot makes it 'free' to move).

The first half of the box step is also called a 'forward box'. The second half of the box or a 'back box' starts with a step backward for the man onto his right foot, a step forward for the lady onto her left foot. The next step is to the side. Left foot for the man, right foot for the woman. On the last step the man brings his right foot back next to his left and the woman takes a step with her left foot.

After completing the steps illustrated in the diagrams, the dancers will be right back where they started, ready for another box step, or any of the other steps of the Waltz. Each of the patterns in this book is complete and lets the dancer 'mix and match' the steps to suit the dancer, the music, or the moment.

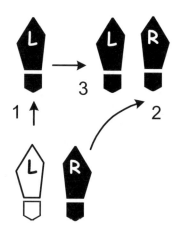

Man's part 1 Waltz Box Step

In Ballroom Dancing all the dance patterns begin with the leader having his weight on his right foot and taking his first step with the left foot. Step one is a comfortable walking step forward. On step two the man's weight should be on the left leg so the right foot is free to take the next step to the side (to the right). Step three with the left foot 'closes' the feet back together. At the end of the 3rd step, the man 'changes weight' to the left foot. This means that after the 3rd step the man is standing with his weight on his left foot so that his right foot is free.

Frequently dance instructors describe the box step as "Forward, Side, Together" or "Forward, Side, Close". Some instructors will call out "Forward, Side, Together, Change Weight" for the benefit of beginners. In the diagrams the weighted foot is shown darker than the unweighted foot at the beginning of the step. As you become more familiar with these steps, the Waltz music makes this pattern nearly effortless as the 1 2 3 1 2 3 tempo dictates one step per beat. Many beginners find Waltz music is the easiest music to dance to because of this.

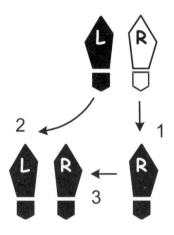

Man's part 2 Waltz Box Step

The second half of the Waltz Box begins with a step backward onto the right foot for the Leader. On step two the man's weight should be on the right leg so the left foot is free to take a step backward and to the left. Step three is to the left with the right foot to 'close' the feet back to the starting position.

Leading Tip: When the man takes a step backward, he should hold his right arm firm. This gently 'pulls' the lady along. It is the job of the man (as the leader) to communicate to the lady what he intends to do. If the man's right arm is limp it does not tell the woman anything and can mislead her.

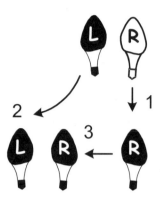

Woman's part 1 Waltz Box Step

Because the man's first step of a pattern is always with the left foot, the woman's first step is always with the right foot. The lady has her weight on the left foot and takes a step backward with the right foot. For step two the woman's weight should be on the right leg so the left foot is free to take a step to her left. Keep pace with the leader and take the right size step. Step three is a step to the left with the right foot to 'close' the feet back together.

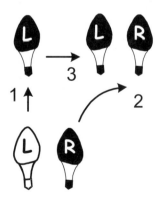

Woman's part 2 Waltz Box Step

The second half of the box is the woman's turn to step forward. The left leg should be free with the weight on the right leg.

When the man takes a step backward, the woman takes a step forward with her left foot. Take a large (or small) enough step to keep the dance frame constant. In other words, take a step that lets you keep the distance the same between yourself and your partner. On step two the woman's weight should be on her left leg so her right foot is free to take a step forward and to the right. Let the man be your guide as to how big a step to take. Step three is a step to the right with the left foot to 'close' the feet back to the starting position.

Following Tip: When the man takes a step forward, the woman's left arm must be firm enough to help her step back and out from under his feet. If the woman's left arm is limp, when the man's body moves forward, the woman's body does not move until the man's body pushes her. This makes it difficult to dance, and looks sloppy. The limp left arm is the biggest reason why women's feet get stepped on. In many cases, when a woman's toes are squashed, it is her own fault for not keeping her left arm firm enough to keep her feet from under her partner!

Variation: Left Turning Box Step

In some old movies you can see Waltz dancers 'spinning' as they dance. What they are doing is a left turning box step: a box step with a turn. On the first beat the man takes a step forward with his left foot and turns it slightly to the left. This causes him to take his side step at a slight angle. On the third beat the man takes a step with his left foot to bring his feet back together. With the second half of the box the man continues the left turn by stepping backward with his right foot and angling his foot to the left.

The side step to the left with the left foot will be at an angle also, and when the right foot 'closes' together with the left, the dancers should be facing 90 degrees (1/4 turn) to the left. Practice this step with more or less turning to see how it feels. You should be able to get a ¼ turn easily and may get as much as a ½ turn (180 degrees) by turning sharply to the left. The turning box is very important because it gives the swirling, spinning look to the Waltz.

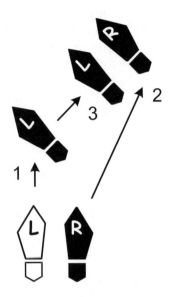

Man's part 1 Left Turning Box Step

The man takes a step forward with his left foot and turns his foot out to his left. Then he takes a step with his right foot to the right side, relative to the new direction he is facing. Then he closes his feet together by taking a step to the right with his left foot.

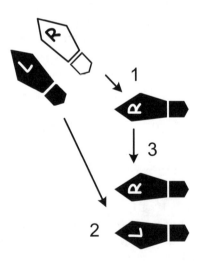

Man's part 2 Left Turning Box Step

The man takes a step back, and turns his foot to his left again. The next step is a step back and to the left side relative to the new direction the man is facing. Then a closing step with the right foot to the left to bring the feet together.

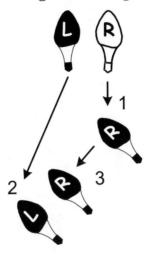

Woman's part 1 Left Turning Box Step

On the first step, the lady steps back as usual, but the left turn of the man will pivot her slightly for the side step and close.

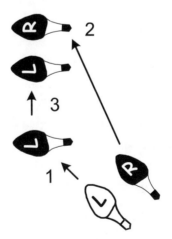

Woman's part 2 Left Turning Box Step

On the first step of the second half of a left turning box the lady will take a step toward her partner and a side step to keep pace with him and maintain the dance frame.

Tip: If you are holding your dance partner properly, with a solid dance frame, she will follow along effortlessly on the left turning box step. If she is not with you at the end of the pattern, try taking smaller steps and turning less sharply. If your dance frame is solid, you will be fine.

Forward Alternate

The second pattern of the Waltz builds on the first and actually reuses the entire first half of the box. The forward alternate is used to advance along the Line of Dance and can be used to move to open space on the dance floor. The Forward Alternate pattern is like a half box step that lets you travel forward along the Line of Dance.

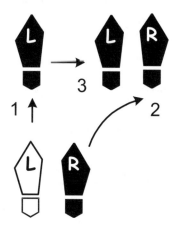

Man's part 1 Forward Alternate

As in the box step, the man takes the first step forward with his left foot. The second step is to the side with the right foot, and the third step is a sidestep with the left foot 'closing' the feet together. At this point it is important to make sure the man changes weight onto his left foot so that he may take his next step with his right foot. Remember: "Forward, Side, Together, Change Weight".

Note: It is possible to steer a course all around the dance floor with the forward alternate; there is no requirement to travel only straight ahead.

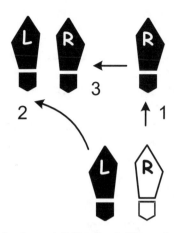

Man's part 2 Forward Alternate

The second half of the forward alternate is a mirror image of the first half. The man takes a step forward with his right foot. Then a step forward and left with his left foot, and finally a side step to the left with his right foot to 'close' the feet together and the leader is back to the starting position, but several feet farther down the Line of Dance.

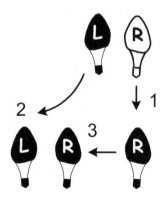

Woman's part 1 Forward Alternate

The Woman's forward alternate is all done with backward steps, because the man is going forward. As the man takes a step with his left foot on the first beat, the woman takes a step backward with her right. Be sure to take a big enough step so your feet are not underneath your partner's feet! Also be careful not to move your feet off to one side in an attempt to avoid being stepped on.

TIP: Take a step backward that lets you touch the floor *after* your partner's foot is planted. As always, a firm left arm will maintain the distance between the dancers and keep the dance frame solid. After the first step backward with the right foot, the lady will take a side step to the left with her left foot, and then a side step left with the right foot to close. Follow your partner's lead and be prepared to move in any direction he chooses to go.

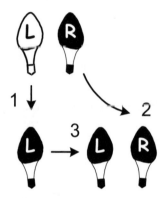

Woman's part 2 Forward Alternate

The second half of the forward alternate has the woman taking a step backward again with her left foot instead of forward as in the box step. After the backward step, the lady takes a step to her right side with her right foot and then a side step right with her left foot to 'close' the feet together. Back, Side, Together, Change Weight, Back, Side, Together, Change Weight... Moving across the dance floor to the music 1 2 3 1 2 3 ...

Waltz Hesitation

Sometimes ballroom dancers can look a tiny bit like bumper cars when the floor gets crowded. Traffic can build in one spot or another into a veritable traffic jam. It is bad form to crash into another couple, and luckily, there are things that can be done to avoid collisions gracefully. One of those things is the Hesitation step. If a couple is waltzing along the Line Of Dance and another couple, for whatever reason, zooms into the space the first couple intended to occupy, a change of plan is required. If a leader can see that the space is already occupied, he can change direction. If it is too late to change direction, he can delay his forward motion for a step by using the Hesitation pattern.

Just as it sounds, the Hesitation involves a pause. The man takes a step forward, just as he would when performing the forward alternate, but instead of taking a side step, he takes a forward step with his left foot, BUT DOES NOT CHANGE WEIGHT to the right foot. With his weight on his left foot, the man 'hesitates' for a beat and DOES NOT change weight to the right foot. After hesitating, the man may then continue forward, or if needed, he may actually take a step back and continue.

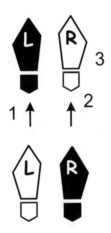

Man's part 1 Hesitation

The illustration shows how simple this pattern is, and this is a good thing when traffic is heavy on the dance floor. On the first beat the man takes a step forward with his left foot. Men always start patterns with the left foot. The second beat has the man taking a step forward with his right foot without putting his weight on it. To remember not to put weight on the right foot, it may help to touch just the toe of the foot to the floor. Beat three has the man 'hesitating' for one count before taking his next step.

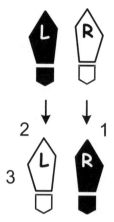

Man's part 2 Hesitation

The second half of the pattern is just like the first half with a backward step instead of a forward step. The man takes a step backward with his right foot on beat one. This is why the man's weight has to be held on the left foot. It is impossible to take a step with the weighted foot! (If you take a step with a weighted foot it is called hopping, not stepping) On the second beat the man takes a step back with his left foot and DOES NOT change weight to that foot. Beat three is another pause where the man touches his toe to the floor and prepares to lead the next pattern. Congratulations! You just avoided a collision and your partner is grateful.

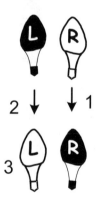

Woman's part 1 Hesitation

The Woman's steps are very similar to the man's steps. On beat one she takes a step backward with her right foot. On beat two she takes a step back with her left foot. It is impossible to read the leader's mind, so putting weight on the left foot is natural. On the third beat when the man hesitates, that is the woman's cue to be prepared to take a step with her left foot, rather than her right foot, so she keeps her weight on her right foot.

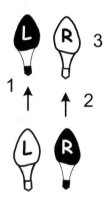

Woman's part 2 Hesitation

The second half is a mirror image of the first half. On beat one, the woman takes a step forward with the left foot. On beat two she takes a step forward with her right foot. On beat three the hesitation lets the woman know to be prepared to take a step with her right foot, so she keeps her weight on the left foot.

Tip: Leaders must make the 'Hesitation' known to their partner. If the step is executed without a clearly defined pause, the lady may not notice the pause and will not have her weight on the correct foot. Exaggerate the pause to make sure she notices.

Waltz Hesitation Left Turn

Dancing in a large ballroom with ample space lets the dancers follow the Line of Dance in a straight line for a long time. When the dancers get to the end of the dance floor, they need to turn the corner and continue along the Line of Dance. The next pattern accomplishes this left turn by combining parts of the two patterns we have already learned. The Hesitation Left Turn combines the first half of the Hesitation with the second half of the Left Turning Box. The result is a flawless method of negotiating corners. This pattern is also an illustration of how the several basic steps in Ballroom Dancing can be combined to generate 'new' patterns.

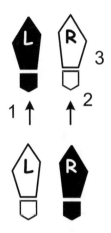

Man's part 1 Hesitation Left Turn

When the couple reach the end of the dance floor, or the leader decides it is time to turn left, the man takes a step forward with his left foot on beat one, forward again with his right foot, and hesitates for the third beat while keeping his weight on the left foot.

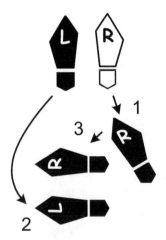

Man's part 2 Hesitation Left Turn

The man takes a step back with his right foot and turns it slightly to the left (counter-clockwise). On the second beat the man takes a step back and to the side, turning the lady with him by holding the dance frame solid. His body motion is enough to lead her through the turn. On the third beat the man takes a step with his right foot to bring his feet back together.

Tip: Be careful not to take steps that are too large. If the man takes a large step it may be difficult for the woman to cover as much ground with a single step. It makes the woman uncomfortable to have to stretch too far, and certainly does not make the couple look elegant.

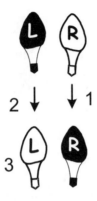

Woman's part 1 Hesitation Left Turn

The woman takes a step back on with her right foot on beat one, back again with the left foot on beat two, and holds her weight on the right leg through the hesitation.

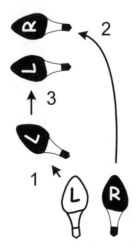

Woman's part 2 Hesitation Left Turn

The woman will feel the man turning on step one and she lets the man guide where her first step will be with her left foot. As always, the lady maintains the dance frame and follows the man as he turns. The second step is a side step with the right foot, and the third step is a side step with the left foot to bring the feet back together.

Putting it together

In this chapter five basic patterns of the Waltz are explained with footprint diagrams to illustrate the steps. Each pattern can be repeated as many times as the leader wants to repeat it, and each pattern can be started from any of the other patterns. Leaders must remember to follow the Line of Dance. Followers must remember to follow the leader! Hesitations can be thrown in whenever traffic dictates, or whenever the leader feels like it. The Left turning basic may be used to add the twirling motion, and may also be used in the corners to change direction. The Hesitation with Left Turn is a more direct method of turning, and may also be used wherever there is space. Mixing and matching these patterns will form a solid foundation for dancing the Waltz at any wedding reception, fund raiser, or ballroom event.

As an example, a couple may start the waltz with the box step, and then move to forward alternates. After two or three forward alternates, the couple executes a hesitation left turn and continues down line of dance with two more forward alternate patterns. The man could then lead a turning box step. The couple continues the left turning box until they are facing line of dance, and then continue down line of dance with the forward alternates. This 'routine' may be continued all around the dance floor. With practice, the patterns will feel natural and comfortable and soon the dancers will be able to talk while dancing! (A major accomplishment in the development of a dancer.)

The Waltz is an excellent first dance to learn because elements of the footwork show up in many of the other dances. Practice often with a partner, or alone with an imaginary partner, until the motions of the box step are second nature.

When "Forward, Side, Close" is effortless, then a dancer is ready to add a touch of style to the Waltz: the up and down motion. If you have ever seen dancers Waltzing in the movies or on the ballroom floor you will notice there is a distinctive 'rise and fall' motion. This is a style point for the Waltz that gives it character. On the '1' beat the dancers will 'rise' up onto the balls of their feet and then 'fall' down to flat feet on the '2' and '3'. The motion should be elegant, and from the feet only. Do not hunch down the shoulders or bob the head up and down. The dance frame should be solid and steady with virtually no movement above the waist. Remember the Waltz is a smooth dance, so float around the ballroom with a subtle rise and fall and you will be impressive.

* * *

Foxtrot

Smooth as silk, graceful and charming, the Foxtrot is the dance where everyone gets to imagine they look like Fred Astair or Ginger Rodgers. If you like Frank Sinatra, Nat King Cole, or Classic Big Band Tunes, this is the dance for you. Remember that the song 'New York, New York' is a Foxtrot. The Foxtrot is a smooth traveling dance that lets you cover a lot of ground. There are simple, elegant patterns, and there are stylish, outrageous patterns, and everything in between. About half of all the Social Music played qualifies as Foxtrot music. This reason alone is enough to learn this dance, but the best reason is that the Foxtrot is easy.

Slow Slow Quick Quick

The Waltz has one and only one way to count the three beats because one beat equals one step. In 4/4 time, when one beat equals one step, it is called a 'March'. Marching is not generally considered 'dancing'. Stepping to the four beats with style leads to dancing the Foxtrot. For a Foxtrot, the beats are counted out in either of two ways depending on the pattern.

The first way to count the beats in the Foxtrot is Slow, Slow, Quick Quick. What this means is that the first step takes two beats. Two beats equals a 'Slow' one beat equals a 'Quick'. The basic Foxtrot pattern follows this timing, and has four steps. There are other Foxtrot patterns that are counted Slow, Quick Quick and take only three steps. The Foxtrot box step follows this timing, and has three steps. For crowded dance floors, tight maneuvering, or a change of pace, this timing is useful. The rest of the time, the Slow Slow Quick Quick timing will get you where you need to go. Remember to look smooth, elegant and graceful, by not moving the upper body too much. Concentrate on balance and don't change directions too quickly at first.

For beginners learning the Foxtrot, think of yourself as striding gracefully to the music. Marching may not be dancing, but if you step to the music with poise you will be fine. Most steps to the Foxtrot are taken just like a regular walking step with the heel touching the floor first. Some steps require the dancers to step only on the ball of the foot, and this will be noted in the foot step diagrams.

Traveling Basic

This step follows the Slow, Slow, Quick Quick count. The dancers start in the closed position where the man has his left foot free (weight on the right foot) and the woman has her right foot free (weight on the left foot).

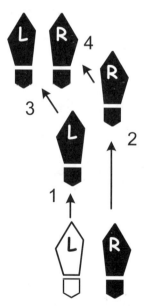

Man's part Foxtrot Traveling Basic

On the first two beats, the man takes a walking step forward with his left foot. (Slow - two beats) On the second two beats the man takes a walking step forward on his right foot. (Slow) On the next beat the man takes a step slightly forward and to the left with his left foot, (Quick - one beat) followed on the next beat by a step slightly forward and left with the right foot (Quick).

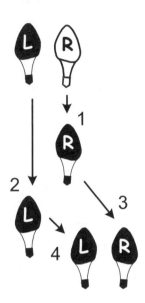

Woman's part Foxtrot Traveling Basic

The woman's part follows the man's in reverse. On the first two beats, (Slow) the lady takes a step backward with her right foot. She should be sure to take a large enough step to keep up with the man's stride. On the second two beats, (Slow) the woman takes a step backward with her left foot. On the next beat (Quick) the lady takes a step backward and to the right with her right foot, and finally on the next beat (Quick) she takes a side step with her left foot to 'close' her feet together.

The traveling basic is a good step to illustrate the value of the 'offset' of a proper dance frame. If the man and the woman are standing "nose-to-nose, toes-to-toes" they are likely to feel knee-to-knee contact with each stride. Be sure to stand two or three inches to the left of center to avoid bruised knees.

Tip: One thing to remember when dancing the Foxtrot, and all other dances for that matter, is to take smaller steps when the music is faster. With less and less time between steps, it really helps to take smaller and smaller steps. It looks more elegant to take small, controlled steps rather than big, sloppy looking steps. Women will appreciate smaller steps because it makes them look more ladylike.

Left Turn

The Foxtrot Left Turn is a very useful step because the Foxtrot is a traveling dance, and when dancers follow the Line Of Dance, eventually they need to turn the corner. The Left Turn lets you do that effortlessly. This pattern is very similar to the Waltz

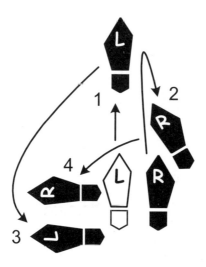

Hesitation Left Turn.

Man's part Left Turn

The man takes a walking step forward on the first beat and waits during the second beat. Remember, two beats is a 'slow', so the first slow step is forward with the left foot. To let the woman know that this is not a basic step pattern, the man should hold his right hand firm on the woman's shoulder blade to let her know not to take another step backward. For the second 'slow' step the man steps backward with a slight turn on his right foot. On the first Quick step the man takes a step to the back and side with his left foot. This should be a very small step because the lady has to keep pace. The man's left foot should be pointing down Line Of Dance along the new wall. At the same time the man is taking this quick step with his left foot, he must bring the lady along with him. Consequently, it makes things easier if this left foot step is small. A giant step here will be awkward for the lady to take, and the man will have to haul her a great distance to maintain the dance frame. So, take a small quick step. The final quick step is with the right foot to close the feet together. The man should be facing down Line Of Dance ready to execute his next pattern.

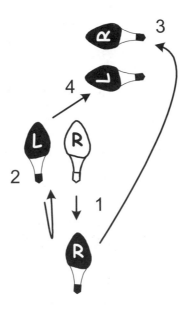

Woman's part Left Turn

The woman takes a step backward with her right foot when she feels the man taking a step forward. The man will be holding the woman's back firmly to let her know that he is not taking another step forward. When the man takes his next step it will be backward, so the woman takes a step forward. Actually, she will be replacing her left foot very close to where it was at the start of the pattern. These two steps are 'slow' steps, taking two beats of music each. The third step is a quick step around the man to the right. The man will be turning, so stay with him and maintain the dance frame. The final quick step is with the left foot to close the feet together.

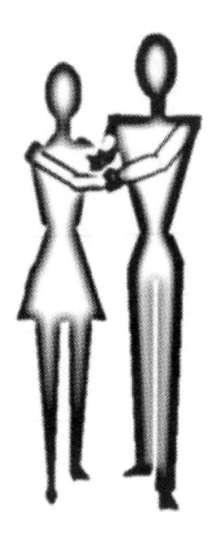

Promenade Position

Promenade Basic

The Promenade Basic has three parts: the intro, the step itself, and the exit. The key to the promenade basic is a change in dance frame (body position) that is accomplished by the leader holding his left arm out in front of his chest rather than off to the side, and adjusting the angle of the dance frame with the right hand. The step itself is done in the 'Promenade' position, which is where the man and woman face toward the Line of Dance at 45 degree angles, so that the man's right shoulder almost touches the woman's left shoulder and both dancers look in the direction they will be traveling.

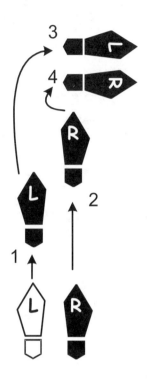

Man's part 1 Promenade Basic

The first task of leading the Promenade basic is to get into promenade position. This is accomplished by leading a variation of the basic step. The two slow steps are straight out of the basic step, and the quick steps are turned to the right ¼ turn clockwise (90 degrees). The man turns the lady as he takes the quick steps.

The man takes a (Slow) step with his left foot, a (Slow) walking step with his right foot and turns 90 degrees to the right with a (Quick) left footed step. The segment finishes with a (Quick) step with the right foot to close the feet together.

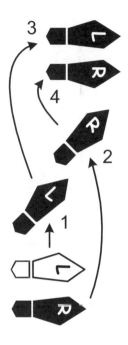

Man's part 2 Promenade Basic

This is the actual 'Promenade' part of the step. The man takes a (Slow) walking step with his left foot diagonally from the direction he is facing. At the same time, he pushes with his left hand, and draws his right hand back to 'tilt' the dance frame so that he is in Promenade Position. His right shoulder should be almost touching the woman's left shoulder, his left arm should be held directly in front of his chest. The second walking step (Slow) continues in the same direction as the first and forces the man's right foot to cross over his left foot. The third step is a (Quick) short step diagonal, and the man turns his foot back to the original direction facing his partner directly. The last step (Quick) brings the man's right foot together with the left and the couple should be in the same position as they started part two of the step.

Tip: Since the leader went to all the trouble to get into this step, it is common to perform the promenade step twice before exiting the step back to the basic step. There are also more advanced steps which can be led from the promenade position, they are covered in the Intermediate Dance Guide.

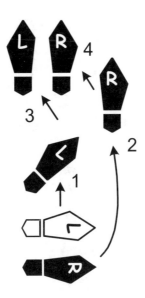

Man's part 3 Promenade Basic

The 'exit' from the promenade basic is simply to resume the basic step. The man takes a (Slow) step forward along the line of dance and turns his foot to the left. At the same time he turns his upper body to face the direction he is moving in. This motion draws the lady around in front of the man again and in line with the steps. The man continues with a (Slow) walking step forward with his right foot, and then a (Quick) step forward and to the left with the left foot and a (Quick) side step with his right foot to close.

The woman starts with her weight on her left foot and she takes a slow step back with her right foot. The next step is another slow step back with the left foot. So far it should be just like a basic step. The two quick steps are turned to the right one quarter turn (90 degrees). Quick right, then quick left. The woman knows to do the quarter turn because the man will be leading her to the promenade position by pushing on her right hand with his left hand and by changing the angle of his right hand on her shoulder blade.

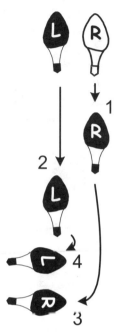

Woman's part 1 Promenade Basic

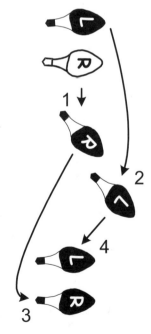

Woman's part 2 Promenade Basic

The next step is a slow step to the side and slightly forward (diagonal) with the right foot. Then another slow step with the left foot crossing in front of the right foot continuing to the side and slightly forward. The next step is a quick step to the side with the right foot and the final quick step is to close the feet together. This is the actual 'promenade' of the promenade position. This may be repeated as many times as the leader wishes.

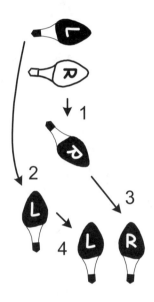

Woman's part 3 Promenade Basic

Exiting the Promenade position is fairly simple. The man will lead the exit by resuming the standard closed frame position which brings the woman around in front of him. To do this, the woman pivots after she takes a slow step to her right with her right foot. The next step is another slow step backward with the left foot. Step three is a quick step to the side and back with the right foot. Step four is a closing step with the left foot.

Fox Box

The Foxtrot also makes use of the box step. In the Foxtrot the rhythm of the step is slightly different than in the Waltz because the time of the music is different. The Waltz uses ¾ time while the Foxtrot uses 4/4 time. The result is that the first step is given two beats for a Slow and the second and third steps each take one beat or Quick Quick. This is the second way to count the four beats of the Foxtrot: Slow Quick Quick. There are a number of steps that use this count in the advanced Foxtrot books.

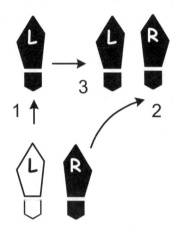

Man's part 1 Foxtrot Box Step

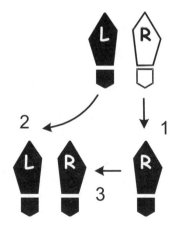

Man's part 2 Foxtrot Box Step

Step one is a comfortable step forward. On Step two the man's weight should be on the left leg so the right foot is free to take the next step to the side (slightly to the right). Step three with the right foot 'closes' the feet back together. At the end of the 3rd step, the man 'changes weight' to the left foot. This means that after the 3rd step the man is standing with his weight on the left foot so that his right foot is free. Frequently dance instructors describe the box step as "Forward, Side, Together" or "Forward, Side, Close". Some instructors will call out "Forward, Side, Together, Change Weight" for the benefit of beginners.

The second half of the Box begins with a step backward onto the right foot for the Leader. On step two the man's weight should be on the right leg so the left foot is free to take a step backward and to the left. Step three is to the left with the right foot to 'close' the feet back to the starting position.

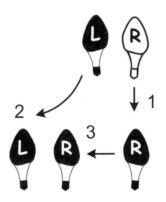

Woman's part 1 Foxtrot Box Step

The lady has her weight on her left foot and takes a step backward with the right foot. Step two the woman's weight should be on the right leg so the left foot is free to take a step to her left. Use your following skill to keep pace with the leader and take the right size step. Step three is a step to the left with the right foot to 'close' the feet back together.

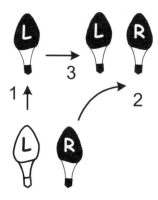

Woman's part 2 Foxtrot Box Step

The second half of the box is the woman's turn to step forward. The left leg should be free with the weight on the right leg. When the man takes a step back, she takes a step forward with her left foot. Take a large (or small) enough step to keep the dance frame constant. In other words, take a step that lets you keep the distance the same between yourself and your partner. On step two the woman's weight should be on her left leg so her right foot is free to take a step forward and to the right. Let the man be your guide as to how big a step to take. Step three is a step to the right with the left foot to 'close' the feet back to the starting position.

Note: the Forward Alternate from the Waltz works here too with the same timing as the Foxtrot box step.

Putting it together

For the Foxtrot we have learned the basic step and the promenade to 'travel' around the dance floor and the left turn to handle the corners. The foxtrot box can be used to avoid collisions or mark time while space clears on the dance floor. It is also easy to use half boxes as a 'forward alternate' to travel with the Slow Quick Quick rhythm. Each of these steps was selected because it can be connected easily to the other steps. The most difficult part will likely be 'shifting gears' from the Slow Slow Quick Quick steps to the Slow Quick Quick steps and back again.

Mix and match these steps until you feel comfortable connecting any of them to any other. Start with the basic traveling step. After three or four basic steps, move to promenade position and do two promenade patterns, throwing in a left turn whenever you need to turn the corner on the dance floor. Shift gears and dance the Fox Box when traffic gets congested. Shift gears back and continue with the Foxtrot traveling basic. Remember, the important part is to have fun and enjoy yourself, the music and your dance partner.

* * *

Tango

The Tango is a smooth dance, and is considered to be one of the most romantic dances. It is certainly intimate, and the reputation of the Tango adds a layer of emotion to the experience. The Tango today is considered elegant and refined, however, it was considered vulgar and scandalous when it was born in Argentina in the late 1800s. There are several historical accounts that describe the Tango starting out as a dance between men! Before 1900, the closed position of the waltz was considered bold, so the tight embrace of the Tango was just too much for polite society. The Tango remained very popular outside of the mainstream, and after many years of refinement, the Tango was finally deemed acceptable to all. Fortunately, the passion of the original dance was retained in many of the poses and patterns of the modern Tango. Tango music is dramatic, colorful and charismatic. Audiences continue to find the Tango alluring and alarming at the same time.

The Tango is a traveling dance, so you will be moving around the dance floor following the Line of Dance. The dance frame for the Tango is like the Waltz or Foxtrot closed position, but the dancers stand closer together with a more fluid body posture than the Waltz or Foxtrot. Keeping both knees flexed throughout the dance allows the dancers to flow smoothly, like a pair of cats. For many of the intermediate and advanced Tango patterns, the dancer's bodies are in greater contact than any other dance. This chapter will cover several basic steps that follow easily from the steps learned in the Waltz and the Foxtrot.

There are three classifications or 'styles' of Tango: American, International, and the Argentine Tango. Some people feel that dancing the Tango is more than just dancing, they refer to Tango as a 'lifestyle'. Needless to say, these people take their Tango *very* seriously. The steps covered in this chapter follow the American Tango style.

Tango Basic Step

The Tango basic step is determined by the music: Slow Slow Quick Quick Slow. Considering there are five steps, this should have the dancers alternating from left foot lead to right foot lead, but the Tango throws in a dash of style to prevent this. On the last Slow step, the dancer drags the foot and does not change weight to the dragged foot. This allows the dancer to take the next step with that same foot, and adds to the character of the dance.

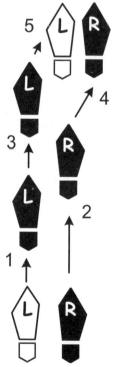

Man's part Tango Basic Step

The man takes a walking step forward with his left foot for two beats (Slow), then a walking step forward with his right foot for two beats (Slow). The third step is a forward walking step (Quick) for one beat, followed by a walking step (Quick) forward and to the right with the right foot. The fifth and final step in the basic pattern is a special step (Slow) forward and to the right with the left foot to close the feet together. For this final step, the man drags his left foot with just the toe touching the dance floor. The man DOES NOT change weight to the left foot. The combination of 'catlike' posture and dragging the foot makes for a dramatic Tango basic step.

Tip: Tango music frequently has a distinctive Slow Slow Quick Quick Slow sound to it. Try to start your basic step on the first of the Slows. It is sometimes easier for beginners to identify the 'Quick Quick Slow', so they listen for it and then start their basic step just after it.

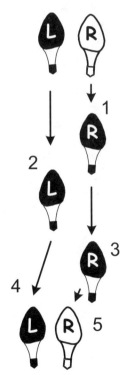

Woman's part Tango Basic Step

The woman's first step (Slow) will be a backward step with the right foot. Be sure to keep the knees flexed and take a large enough step backward, but try not to lunge away from your partner. Next will be a backward step (Slow) with the left foot. The third step is a backward step (Quick) with the right foot and then a step (Quick) back and to the left with the left foot. The fifth and final step will be a (Slow) drag of the right foot. The key to this

Tango Corte' Pose

step is to NOT change weight to the right foot. Stay close to your partner, keep your knees flexed, and enjoy the drama that is the Tango.

Tip: Tango music is fairly distinctive, and you may find that your partner did not start on the proper beat. Ignore this error.

Tango music is written in 4/4 time, so the steps will work even if the emphasis of the music is not synchronized with your leader. It is generally more enjoyable to dance than to point out a beginner's mistakes.

Tango Corte'

The Corte' is a pose the dancers strike as well as a pattern. There are other dances that use the Corte', but it has 'Tango' written all over it.

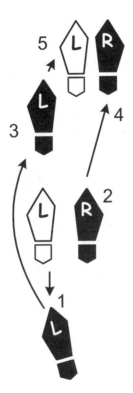

Man's part Corte'

The first step of the Corte' pattern is a backward (Slow) step with the left foot. The left foot is turned slightly outward to make it easier to bend the knee. The right leg stays relatively straight, and the dancers 'settle' into the Corte pose and then gracefully rise out of it on the next step. The second step is a (Slow) step putting the dancer's weight back onto the right foot. There is no real step taken, but the weight change allows the third step to be taken (Quick) forward with the left foot. The next step is a step forward and to the right with the right foot, followed by the Tango Close step, which is a foot drag step with the left foot. Again, do not change weight to the left foot on this final step. The Corte' pattern can be thought of as the first half consisting of the actual Corte', followed by the Quick Quick Slow (Forward Side Close) of the Tango Basic.

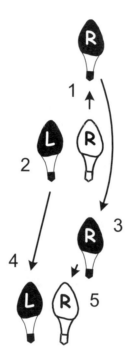

Woman's part Corte'

The woman's first step of the Corte' is a forward step with the right foot. The man will bend his knee, lowering himself slightly, so the woman may lean into him for the Corte' pose. It is advisable not to put too much (if any) weight on your partner. It will be easier for the woman to take her next step if she is supporting her own weight, rather than leaning on her partner. The next step is a step back onto the left foot. This foot may actually not have moved from where the woman started the pattern. By the end of the second (Slow) step, the dancers are out of the Corte' pose and ready to move. The third step is a (Quick) backward step with the right foot, followed by a (Quick) step back and to the left with the left foot. The final step of the Corte' is a (Slow) dragging step back and to the left with the right foot where only the toe of the foot touches the floor. Do not change weight to the right foot, keep it free for the first step of the next pattern.

Tango Promenade

The Tango Promenade is a favorite of the women because they get to show off. The Promenade steps for the man are very similar to the basic step, but for the woman, there is a dramatic half turn with flair. The dancers start out in the closed position, but assume the promenade position with the first step. The second step is a promenade step for the man, but a half pirouette for the woman. From there on the pattern conforms to the Tango Basic.

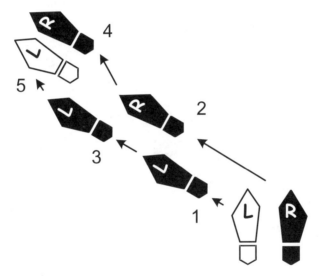

Man's part Tango Promenade

The Tango Promenade pattern begins from the closed position, but immediately shifts to the promenade position, which means the man and woman both face forward (Line Of Dance) with the man's right shoulder close to the woman's left shoulder. The man takes a step (Slow) to the left and slightly forward with his left foot. The second (Slow) step is a promenade step forward with the right foot. While the man is taking this step, the man must turn (pivot) the woman to the closed position. The woman will take a (Slow) promenade step, and with the help of the man, then pivot from the promenade position to the closed position. The Third step is a (Quick) forward step with the left foot, then a step (Quick) forward and to the right with the right foot and then a (Slow) close with the left foot dragging together with no change of weight. This pattern can be used to turn corners on the dance floor.

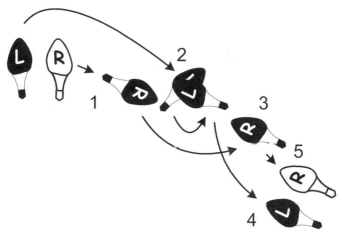

Woman's part Tango Promenade

Just as the man begins the pattern from the closed position, so does the woman. But the dancers immediately shift to the promenade position where both the man and the woman face forward (Line Of Dance) with the woman's left shoulder close to the man's right shoulder. The woman follows the man with a step (Slow) to her right with her right foot. The second (Slow) step is a promenade step forward with the left foot and the woman pivots counter-clockwise from promenade position to closed position. The man uses his right arm and left hand to help the woman turn to the closed position in one smooth motion. The third step (Quick) is taken directly backward with the right foot, then a (Quick) step backward and to the left with the left foot and then a (Slow) close with the right foot dragging together with no change of weight.

Tango Rocks

This next pattern plays with the timing of the Tango and introduces rocking steps. The timing of the Tango, as stated before, is Slow Slow Quick Quick Slow. The Tango Rocks pattern takes one of the Slow steps and breaks it into two Quick steps. Because a Slow is two beats and a Quick is one beat, the math works out fine. This pattern is a good test for the man's leading skills because he will be doing something that the woman can not anticipate. It is also a good test for the woman's following skills because she will have to do what her partner does, not what she expects him to do.

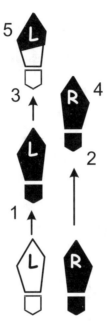

Man's part 1 Tango Rocks

The pattern starts out just like a Tango basic with a step (Slow) forward with the left foot, followed by a (Slow) step forward with the right foot. On the third step (Quick) the man takes a rocking step forward. What this means is that the man does not take a walking step forward and put all his weight on the left foot, rather, he touches only the ball of the foot to the floor and rocks forward onto the foot, ready to rock back immediately. The fourth step (Quick) is a rocking step backward onto the right foot. The right foot does not actually move much (if at all) but the rocking back and forth motion puts the man's weight on the right foot. The man should be sure to hold the lady firmly with his right hand on her shoulder blade so she does not continue backwards as in a basic Tango step. The fifth step (Slow) is a walking step forward onto the left foot.

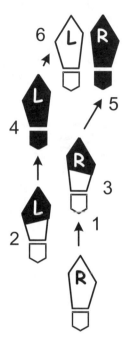

Man's part 2 Tango Rocks

Now comes the tricky part. The first half of the Tango Rocks followed the Slow Slow Quick Quick Slow rhythm, but the second half breaks the first Slow into two Quicks. The result is that the steps follow a Quick Quick Slow Quick Quick Slow pattern. Six steps rather than five. The first step (Quick) is a forward rocking step with the right foot. Because it is a rocking step, the next step (Quick) rocks back onto the left foot. The third step is a (Slow) walking step forward on the right foot. The last three steps are the same as the last three steps of the Tango Basic: step (Quick) forward with the left, step (Quick) forward and to the right with the right foot and close (Slow) by dragging the left foot forward and to the right bringing the feet together with the weight still on the right foot.

Editor's note: The foot prints show the rock step on step one, but do not show the walking step on step three. The walking step is there, it just can not be shown without covering the rock step in the diagram.

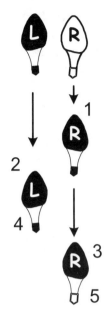

Woman's part 1 Tango Rocks

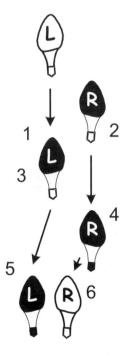

Woman's part 2 Tango Rocks

The woman's part 1 first two steps are just like the Tango Basic. The first step (Slow) is a backward step with the right foot, followed by a backward step (Slow) with the left foot. The third step is a backward step (Quick) with the right foot but the next step (Quick) is FORWARD with the left foot. There is little movement of the left foot, it is more like replacing one's weight onto the foot. The fifth step is a (Slow) step backward with the right foot. Keep your knees flexed and be alert to the steps your partner actually takes, not the ones you expect him to take.

The rock step in the first half should make the woman alert to unexpected steps, and they are taken immediately in the woman's part 2 of the Tango Rocks pattern. The first Slow step in the second half of the pattern is broken into two Quick steps. Consequently, the first step (Quick) is a backward rocking step with the left foot. Because it is a rocking step, the next step (Quick) rocks forward onto the right foot. The third step is a (Slow) walking step backward with the left foot. The last three steps are the same as the last three steps of the Tango Basic: step (Quick) backward with the right, step (Quick) backward and to the left with the left foot and close (Slow) by dragging the right foot backward and to the left to bring the feet together, keeping the weight on the left foot.

Putting it together

For the Tango we have learned the basic step, the Corte' and the Tango Rocks to travel around the dance floor.   It is possible to use the basic step or the Promenade step to turn the corners as well. The Corte can be used to add spice, avoid collisions, or mark time while space clears on the dance floor. Each of these steps was selected because it can be connected easily to the other steps. The most difficult part will likely be starting out on the right beat to catch the distinctive Tango steps. Listen for the Quick Quick Slow, and be ready to start off immediately after it. Mix and match these steps until you feel comfortable connecting any of them to any other pattern. Start with the basic traveling step. After three or four basic steps, throw in a promenade, or do two promenade patterns to turn the corner. From there try the Tango Rocks to mix up the beat a little. Whenever traffic gets heavy, use the Corte. Remember the scandalous origins of the Tango, enjoy yourself, the music and your dance partner.

* * *

Night Club Two Step

The Night Club Two Step is a relatively new dance that goes well with Soft Rock, Pop and slower contemporary tunes. For all the songs that are slow dance songs, where other couples are doing the 'Penguin Shuffle' or the 'Clutch and Sway', the Night Club Two Step is a dance that can set you apart from the crowd. It is a good dance for beginners because the footwork is straight forward and lets the dancers relax and enjoy moving to the music.

There are differing opinions about the best way to teach this dance, and differing opinions about how it should be performed. Some schools teach this dance starting with the rock-step to emphasize the rhythm dance element. Other schools teach the Night Club Two Step starting with the slow step to the side to emphasis the smooth element. Either way has its merits, but this book will illustrate the steps starting with the smooth side step. One thing is certain: the Night Club Two Step is a spot dance. Dancers do not travel the Line of Dance with this dance.

The basic step in this dance is a slow step to the side, sometimes described as a 'skating' step because of the similar movement to ice skating. The side step is followed by a rock-step and replace. It is important that the rock-step be taken behind the weighted foot, but dancers should be careful not to twist at the hip or waist. If the dancer's hips are not square with their partner's hips, the rock-step is too far behind the weighted foot.

NCTS Basic Step

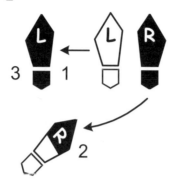

Man's part 1 Basic Step

Starting in the closed dance frame position, the first step of the man's basic step is a (Slow) step to the left with the left foot. This should not be a small step in terms of distance, but it should not be too large a step for the woman to comfortably follow. This step is sometimes described as a 'skating' step because of the similarity to the motion of ice skating. The next step is a (Quick) rock step back on to the right foot. The right foot should be behind the left foot, about even with the left heel. This step is a quick rock back, but it is important that the man put his weight on the right foot for just a moment in order to get the proper look and feel of this dance step. The man then replaces his weight on to his left foot by taking a (Quick) step in place with his left foot.

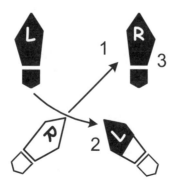

Man's part 2 Basic Step

The second half of the basic step is a mirror image of the first part. The man takes a (Slow) skating step to the right with his right foot, then a (Quick) rock step back on his left foot behind his right foot, and then a (Quick) step replacing the weight on his right foot.

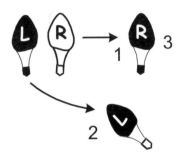

Woman's part 1 Basic Step

The woman takes a (Slow) step to the right with her right foot, then a (Quick) rock step back on her left foot behind her right foot, and then a (Quick) step replacing the weight on her right foot.

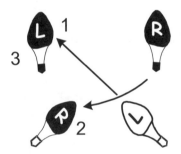

Woman's part 2 Basic Step

The woman takes a (Slow) step to the left with her left foot, then a (Quick) rock step back on her right foot behind her left foot, and then a (Quick) step replacing the weight on her left foot.

Lady's Under Arm Turn

This is a very good pattern for the woman to learn because it is essentially the same foot work that is used in the Salsa, Cha-cha, and Rumba under arm turns. The pattern is excellent for the man to learn because it is almost effortless and adds a great deal to the visual appeal of the dance and the enjoyment of the dancers.

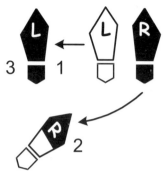

Man's part 1 Lady's Under Arm Turn

The man dances the same steps as he does in the basic step while he leads the woman through the turn. To prepare for the turn, the man must release his right hand from the woman's shoulder blade to allow her to turn. This also gives the woman advance warning that a turn is coming. While dancing the basic step, the man lets go with his right hand to prepare for the turn. The diagram shows the steps the man takes, and assumes the man has released his right hand already in preparation. The man then takes a (Slow) step to the left with his left foot and raises his left hand (and consequently the woman's right hand) up about two inches above the woman's head. The man can also make a small clockwise circle motion with his left hand. The man then takes a (Quick) rock step back on to his right foot as the woman turns, and then he replaces his weight on to his left foot as he lowers his left hand.

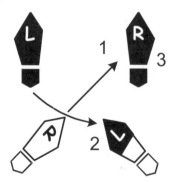

Man's part 2 Lady's Under Arm Turn

The woman's turn is complete at this point, so the man takes a (Slow) step to the right with his right foot so that he can resume the dance frame with his partner. The couple uses the second half of the pattern to return to the closed dance frame position. The man then takes a (Quick) rock step back on his left foot and then a (Quick) weight replace onto his right foot.

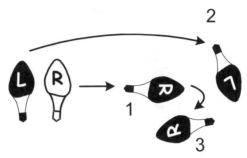

Woman's part 1 Lady's Under Arm Turn

The woman takes a (Slow) step to the right with her right foot as the man raises her right hand over her head. This is a clockwise turn, so the woman takes her next (Quick) step to the right with her left foot and pivots 180 degrees to face back where she came from. The pivot happens on the second quick and results in the woman's weight being on her right foot. This allows her to take the next step with her left foot to the left to continue the basic step and resume the dance frame. The man will lower his hand at the end of the turn.

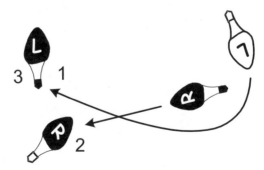

Woman's part 2 Lady's Under Arm Turn

The woman has completed her turn and her weight is on her right foot. The woman then takes a (Slow) step to the left with her left foot as the man closes the frame. The woman then takes a

(Quick) rock step back on to her right foot and then a (Quick) step replacing her weight on to her left foot.

Left Turning Basic

This pattern allows the man to lead the woman to turn left and lets the dancers travel to another spot on the dance floor.

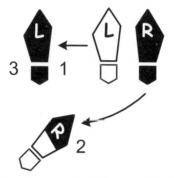

Man's part 1 Left Turning Basic

The man starts by leading the first half of the Two Step basic step: Slow step left with left foot, quick rock back with right foot, quick replace on left foot.

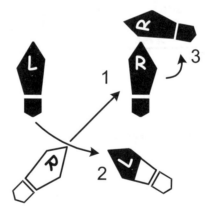

Man's part 2 Left Turning Basic

The man then takes a slow step to the right with his right foot and twists his upper body to the left (counter-clockwise). This indicates to the woman that the couple is turning. The man uses the next step, a quick rock back with the left foot, to turn his body 90 degrees to the left (counter-clockwise) from the direction he started. The man then takes a replace step (Quick) with the right foot turned at least 90 degrees to prepare for the next step. While the man is doing this, he is maintaining the dance frame so the woman is turning with him.

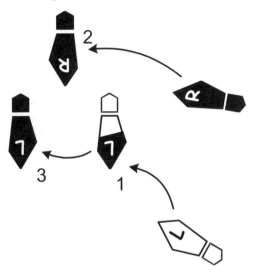

Man's part 3 Left Turning Basic

The next step is a slow step forward and to the man's right, but turning the left foot towards the left. This step turns the dancers another 90 degrees so that the man is now facing the direction the woman was facing when he started this pattern. The man then takes a (Quick) step to the right with his right foot. The

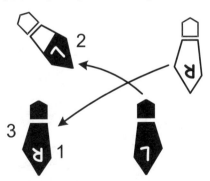

Man's part 4 Left Turning Basic

man should be careful to place his right foot behind his left foot so he can take the next step with his left foot in front of his right foot. The man then takes a (Quick) step to the left with his left foot. This is known as a 'Buzz Step'. This may look like an awkward position in the diagram, but the steps flow smoothly on the dance floor and there is no pause here.

For the fourth part, the man then takes a (Slow) step to the right with his right foot, then a (Quick) rock step back with his left foot and then replaces the weight (Quick) on his right foot. This should be recognizable as the basic step of the Night Club Two Step, and the dancers have successfully executed a left turn!

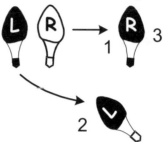

Woman's part 1 Left Turning Basic

The woman follows the man's lead and dances the first half of the basic step: (Slow) step right with the right foot, (Quick) rock step back with the left foot and a (Quick) replace with the right foot.

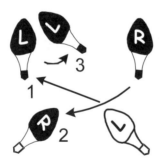

Woman's part 2 Left Turning Basic

The man will begin to twist his body as he takes the next step. The woman responds to this by taking a (Slow) step to the left with her left foot which is comfortable and allows for the turn the man is introducing. The woman then takes a (Quick) rock step back with her right foot and replaces her weight (Quick) on her left foot while turning her left foot to the left 90 degrees.

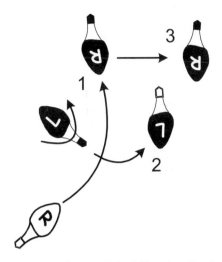

Woman's part 3 Left Turning Basic

The man is turning around the woman at this point, so the woman takes her next (Slow) step with her right foot forward and to the right as she pivots on her left foot. The woman is now facing in the direction the man was facing when the pattern started. The woman then takes a (Quick) step to the left with her left foot, and a (Quick) step to the left with her right foot. The woman should be careful to place her right foot behind her left foot. This is a buzz step.

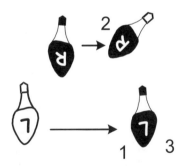

Woman's part 4 Left Turning Basic

The woman then takes a (Slow) step to the left with her left foot, followed by a (Quick) rock step back on the right foot, and then a (Quick) replace step with the left foot and the couple is back to the basic step facing a new direction.

Lady's Outside Turn

This pattern emphasizes the rhythm elements of the Night Club Two Step. The Lady's Outside Turn is very much like a swing dance move, but the timing is slowed down to match the music. From the basic step, the man separates from the closed position to the open position where he then leads the woman to turn counter-clockwise while 'changing places' with her. That is, after the turn, the man is standing where the woman started the pattern, and vice versa. This pattern combines elements from the other steps into a simple yet elegant turn.

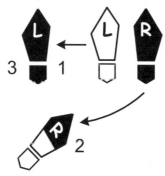

Man's part 1 Lady's Outside Turn

The man leads the basic step and as he does so, he releases his right hand from the woman's shoulder blade and slides his hand along her arm until he takes her left hand in his right hand. This is the open position of the Night Club Two Step.

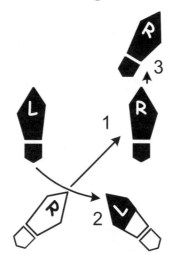

Man's part 2 Lady's Outside Turn

From the open position, the man releases the woman's left hand as he takes a (Slow) step to the right with his right foot. Then the man gently pushes the woman backward as he takes his rocking (Quick) step back with his left foot. As the man replaces his weight on his right foot, he takes a small step forward and pulls the woman forward. As he pulls the woman forward, he draws his left hand across his chest and up towards his right ear. Drawing the woman's right hand up and across is the signal to her that she will be turning counter-clockwise.

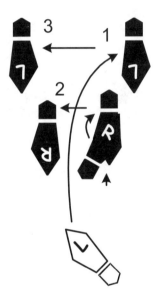

Man's part 3 Lady's Outside Turn

As the woman turns counter-clockwise, the man pivots on his right foot and takes a (Slow) step back and away from the woman with his left foot. This should put the man in the spot where the lady started the pattern. The woman should be finished with her turn now, so the man lowers his left hand (and the lady's right hand) and takes a buzz step to the man's right. The Buzz step consists of a (Quick) step to the right with the right foot and a (Quick) step to the right with the left foot behind the right foot.

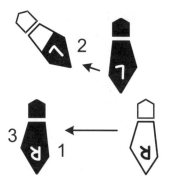

Man's part 4 Lady's Outside Turn

The man then takes a (Slow) skating step to the right with the right foot and resumes the closed dance frame with the lady as he takes his (Quick) rock step with the left foot, and then replaces his weight on the right foot (Quick).

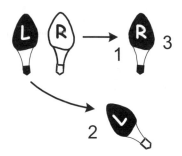

Woman's part 1 Lady's Outside Turn

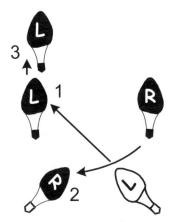

Woman's part 2 Lady's Outside Turn

For the woman's part 1 the footwork is identical to the basic step: (Slow) skating step to the right with the right foot, then a (Quick) rock back on the left foot, then (Quick) replacing the weight on the right foot. However, the first thing the leader has to do to lead this pattern is to get into the open position, so the man will release his hand from the woman's shoulder blade and slide it down her left arm. The woman holds on to the man's right hand while continuing the basic step

For the woman's part 2, now in the open position, the woman takes a (Slow) step to the left with the left foot, then a (Quick) rock back on the right foot, when the woman should feel the leader pulling her to step forward. So the woman steps forward as she replaces the weight on her left foot.

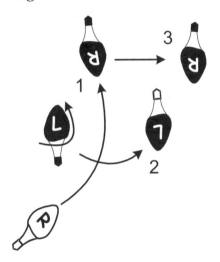

Woman's part 3 Lady's Outside Turn

The man will be raising the woman's right hand up over her head at this point, which is the indication that the woman should turn. This turn is a counter-clockwise pivot on the left foot which results in the woman facing the opposite direction from where she started the turn.

As the woman turns, the man passes behind her so he is standing where she started the turn. After her pivot turn, the woman should be standing where the man was standing. The pivot turn includes a (Slow) step with the right foot, which is followed by a buzz step: a (Quick) step to the left with the left foot and then a (Quick) step to the left with the right foot behind the left foot. The man will lower his left hand and lead the buzz step left.

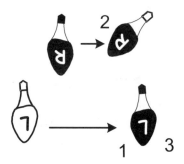

Woman's part 4 Lady's Outside Turn

After the buzz step, the woman finishes the pattern with a (Slow) step to the left with the left foot, then a (Quick) rock step back with the right foot, and then a (Quick) step replaces her weight on her right foot. The leader may resume the closed position dance frame here, or he may lead another step from the open position.

Putting it together

The Night Club Two Step moves can be combined in pretty much any order. Start with the basic step, and when you feel comfortable with that, add the Lady's under arm turn. Follow that up with two more basic steps and then a Lady's outside turn. Dance two more basic steps and then lead the left turning basic. When you are really comfortable with the patterns, combine the Lady's Under Arm Turn with the Lady's outside turn. When the music is slow, dance the Two Step as a slow romantic dance instead of the Penguin Shuffle. When the music is faster, emphasize the rhythm elements of the dance and use the Two step instead of a slow swing dance. Above all, feel the music and enjoy the dance. Mix and match these steps and have a good time.

* * *

Swing

Swing dancers were once described as 'Jitterbugs'. The name stuck, and remains a synonym for The Swing. As it turns out, Swing Dances cover a lot of ground both literally and figuratively. There are many distinct styles of swing dancing including (but not limited to!) the East Coast Swing, the West Coast Swing, the Lindy, the Hustle, Boogie-woogie dancing and even Jive dancing. Swing dancing can be very casual and calm when danced by veterans of W.W.II, but it can also be athletic and almost acrobatic at dance competitions. The Swing is a spot dance, and it is characterized by the couple rocking back away from each other before or after each pattern.

West Coast vs. East Coast Swing

East Coast Swing (ECS) is possibly the easiest Swing dance to learn. It has many six and eight count patterns that allow the couple to rotate around each other without worrying too much about space, direction, or orientation. ECS is a free form dance where the man and woman are free to change places, move around each other, and improvise in all directions.

The West Coast Swing (WCS) on the other hand has a few strict rules. WCS uses a 'slot' which is an imaginary runway where the woman moves back and forth in a straight line. The man leads the woman from one end of the slot to the other and steps around her and out of her way as she moves from one end of the slot to the other and back. There are similar patterns in both ECS and WCS, but the WCS must observe the 'slot'.

Swing patterns have several different ways to count the steps. As mentioned above, there are six count patterns, and eight count patterns (as well as other counts that will not be covered in this chapter). What this means is that the dancers count their steps using six or eight beats of music. A six count pattern is counted as One (Quick) Two (Quick) Three-And-Four (triple step) Five-And-Six (triple step) where the rock back is on one, the replace is on two and the triple steps follow as Three-And-Four, Five-And-Six. The dancers take eight steps, but count to six because of the 'AND' counts for the triple steps. What is a triple step? Not surprisingly, a triple step is a combination of three steps taken in quick succession: Left-Right-Left or Right-Left-Right. The foot print diagrams will make everything clear, but for now just know that the most important thing about a triple step is that the dancer ends up with the correct foot free to take the next step.

An eight count pattern is counted as One (Quick) Two (Quick) Three-And-Four (triple step) Five (Quick) Six (Quick) Seven-And-Eight (triple step) where the rock back is on one, the replace is on two. The triple step is then followed by two more quick steps (which may or may not include a rock step) followed by a triple step to finish the pattern. The dancers take ten steps, but count to eight because of the 'AND' counts for the triple steps.

Just like the other dances, to start out it may help to count the beats and steps out loud. Swing dances look effortless, simple, and straightforward when accomplished dancers perform them, but the timing and coordination require great concentration until it becomes familiar.

When the music is relatively slow, it is possible to take larger steps and move around quite a bit. As the pace of the music gets faster and faster it becomes necessary to shrink the size of the steps. A good rule of thumb for dancing is — the faster the music, the smaller the steps. When dancing Swing patterns it is a good idea to remain light on your feet. Dance on the balls of your feet and you will be better able to keep up.

Another element that sets the Swing Dances apart is the 'Dance Posture'. Swing Dance Posture is a much more athletic posture than the smooth ballroom dance posture. Swing dancers tend to keep their knees flexed, leaning from the waist is necessary at times, and the arms are used occasionally for balance. Because the link between the dancers is often times just their hands, it is very important that the connection be solid. The proper way to hold hands in the Swing dances is to make a 'cup' with the hand, and a 'hook' with the fingers. The thumbs have no use in Swing dancing, so it is best to keep them out of the way. Lay them down flat next to the index fingers and forget about them for a while. After the dancers make cups and hooks out of their hands, the proper link is made by the man holding his hand(s) with the palm up. Women hold their hand(s) with the palm down. Occasionally this is temporarily reversed, but the starting position is always with the man's palms up.

With all the twisting and turning that the dancers do, it is sometimes tempting to grab on with the thumbs. This is always a bad idea. When one partner grabs onto the other partner's hand it is impossible to execute a turn. The arm twists only so far, and it is possible to injure yourself or your partner if you do not let go during a turn. Use the hook position for the hand, and during the turn, the hook to hook connection turns into a 'ball and socket' connection. The man's fingers form the ball, and the woman's palm forms the socket. This allows free movement during the turns, and no risk of injury.

Some things never change, however, and the man will be starting each of the following patterns with his left foot, and the woman will be starting all the patterns with her right foot. Another thing that never changes is that the dancers must hold their arms firm. If the leader or the follower have 'noodle arms' the dancers look sloppy and the patterns are much more difficult to execute.

East Coast Swing

ECS Basic

The basic step for the Swing is a triple step to the left for the man, then a triple step to the right, then a rock step back on the left foot. The Basic step can be done in the closed position, half open position, or the open position.

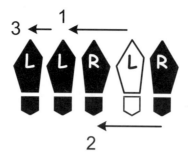

Man's part 1 ECS Basic

The man begins with his weight on his right foot so his left foot is free. The first step of the triple step is taken sideways to the left with the left foot on the first beat. The second step is taken with the right foot sideways between beats 1 and 2. The third step is with the left foot again, stepping sideways to the left on the 2nd beat. It helps in the beginning to count the steps out loud by saying 'Tri-ple-Step' where the first step is on Tri, the second step is on 'ple' and the third step is on 'step'.

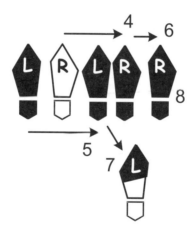

Man's part 2 ECS Basic

The second part of the swing basic starts with a step to the right with the right foot on the 3rd beat, then a step to the right with the left foot between the 3rd and 4th beats, followed by a step to the right with the right foot on the 4th beat. Then the man takes a rocking step back with his left foot on the 5th beat and replaces his weight on the right foot on the 6th beat. To count the steps use "3 AND 4, 5, 6" where '3' is the first step right, 'AND' is the second step, '4' is the third step, '5' is the rock back and '6' is replacing the weight on the right foot.

Note: Leading the Swing is different from the smooth dances because the frame is different. The contact with the lady is almost entirely through the arms. Keep your arms firm, your fingers 'cupped' and keep your thumbs out of the way.

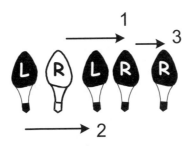

Woman's part 1 ECS Basic

As you might expect, the woman's part mirrors the man's part. The woman starts with her weight on the left foot and takes a step to the right with her right foot on the first beat. The next step is to the right with the left foot between beats 1 and 2, and the third step is with the right foot to the right on the 2nd beat. To count the steps use '1 AND 2' where the first step is on '1', the second step is on 'AND' and the third step is on '2'.

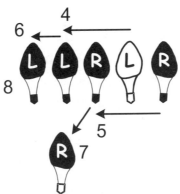

Woman's part 2 ECS Basic

The second part starts with a step to the left with the left foot on the 3rd beat, then a step to the left with the right foot between the 3rd and 4th beats, and then a step to the left with the left foot on the 4th beat. Then the woman takes a rocking step backward with the right foot on the 5th beat and replaces her weight on the left foot on the 6th beat. To count the steps use '3 & 4, 5, 6' where '3' is the first step left, 'AND' is the second step, '4' is the third step left, '5' is the rock back and '6' is replacing the weight on the left foot.

ECS Lady's Under Arm Turn

This is the classic swing pattern where the couple 'swap places' with the Lady turning counter-clockwise. Each dancer uses the first triple step to turn, then the second triple step is done facing each other and finally the rock step to launch into the next pattern.

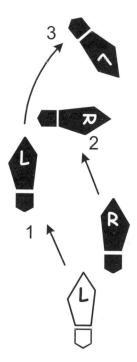

Man's part 1 ECS Lady's Under Arm Turn

The man takes the first step of his triple step forward with his left foot as he raises his left hand (and consequently the woman's right hand) up and across his body towards his right ear. This will lead the woman in a counter-clockwise turn. The second step is forward with his right foot as he turns 90 degrees. The man should be facing the woman throughout the turn. The third step of the triple step is taken with the left foot and turns another 90 degrees. At this point the man's arm should be back down at waist level after turning the woman.

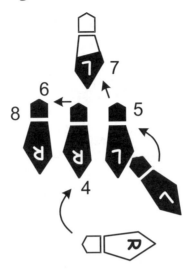

Man's part 2 ECS Lady's Under Arm Turn

The next triple step is taken with the man traveling slightly to his right. The first step of the second triple step is with his right foot completing the turn to face the woman (4). The next step is with his left foot lining up with his right foot (5), and the third step in the triple is with the right foot stepping to the right (6). This is followed by the rock step back on the left foot (7), and replacing the weight on the right foot (8), ready for the next pattern.

For her part 1, the woman takes a step forward with her right foot (1) as the man leads the turn by raising the woman's right hand. The woman then turns counter-clockwise to her left, stepping with her left foot(2). The third step of the triple step is taken with her right foot at the completion of her turn (3).

Part 2 has the woman traveling slightly to her left as she takes the second triple step. The first step in the second triple step is taken with the left foot as she completes the turn and faces her partner (4). The next step is taken to her left with the right foot (5), and the final step of the second triple is taken with

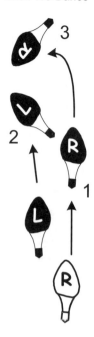

Woman's part 1 ECS Lady's Under Arm Turn

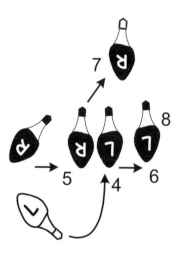

Woman's part 2 ECS Lady's Under Arm Turn

the left foot to the left (6). Then the woman rocks back onto her right foot (7), and replaces her weight on her left foot (8) and is ready for the next pattern.

ECS Cut Through

This pattern has the man turning counter-clockwise while the woman passes by on his right. The man passes the woman's left hand behind his back as he turns; taking it in his right hand and then taking it back again with his left hand after his turn. The footwork for the man is simple, and the footwork for the woman is even easier.

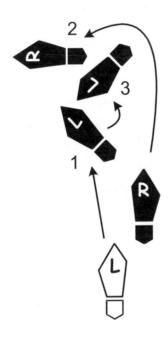

Man's part 1 ECS Cut Through

The man takes a step forward and to his left with his left foot on the first triple step. As he does this he pulls the woman's right hand toward his right hip. Do not pull her hand upwards or she will think she is supposed to turn! The man takes the woman's right hand with his right hand as he takes his second step, forward and left with his right foot. The third step of the first triple is with the left foot as the man takes the woman's right hand back into his left hand. At this point the man should have turned 90+ degrees and be holding his partner's right hand in his left hand.

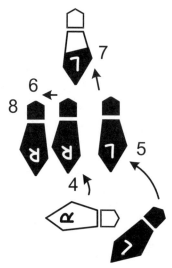

Man's part 2 ECS Cut Through:

The second triple step starts with a step to the right with the right foot so the man is facing his partner. The next step is to the right with the left foot, and then a step to the right with the right foot to finish the triple step. Then the man takes a rock step back with his left foot and replaces his weight on his right foot, ready to lead the next pattern.

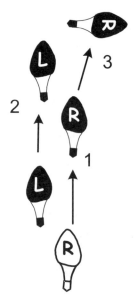

Woman's part 1 ECS Cut Through:

The woman takes a step forward with her right foot, then a step forward with her left foot, then a step forward with a quarter turn with her right foot to finish the triple step. While she is taking these steps, the man takes her hand and passes it behind his back as he turns.

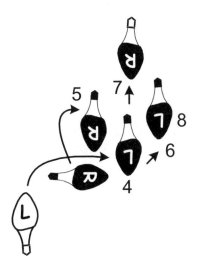

Woman's part 2 ECS Cut Through:

At this point the man has turned around to face the woman and leads her to take a triple step to her left. Left foot first, turning to face the man squarely, then a step to the left with the right foot, then a step to the left with the left foot to complete the second triple step. Then the woman takes a rock step back on her right foot and replaces her weight on the left foot, ready to follow the next pattern.

Putting It Together

The East Coast Swing basic is the place to start. Dance this step until it feels comfortable and natural to take the triple steps to the left and right. Feel the music as you shuffle to the left and shuffle to the right. When you are ready, use the rock step to launch into the next pattern. The Lady's Under Arm Turn will make you feel like you are swing dancing. Alternate between the basic step and the Lady's Under Arm Turn a few times and then try the cut through. The cut through will give the man a chance to turn and let the lady take a break. When these moves feel comfortable, mix them up in any order, or do them in pairs.

West Coast Swing

WCS Basic

Some Dance instructors believe it is easier to start dancing the West Coast Swing basic step starting with the triple step, so they add a 'starter step' consisting of two triple steps. Others feel it is better to start the dance step with the rock step so the steps can be taught from a consistent starting point. The rock step is a very consistent part of the WCS, and can be a good reference point for beginning dancers. Try adding two triple steps as a 'starter step' and see how it feels. Then use the one that feels best to you.

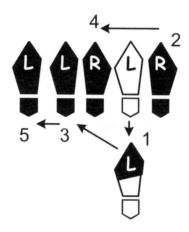

Man's part 1 WCS Basic

The couple starts in the open or half open position, and the man's weight is on his right foot with his left foot free. The first step is a rock back with the left foot on the first beat. The second step is replacing his weight on the right foot on beat two. The third step is a step to the left with the left foot on beat three. Step four is a step to the left with the right foot in between beats 3 and 4. Step five is a step left with the left foot on beat four. Count the steps as: One, Two, Three And Four.

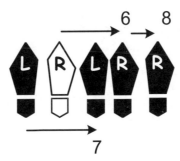

Man's part 2 WCS Basic

The second half of the WCS Basic has the man taking a step to the right with the right foot on beat 5, then a step to the right with the left foot between beats 5 and 6, and then a step to the right with the right foot on beat 6. Count the steps as: Five And Six.

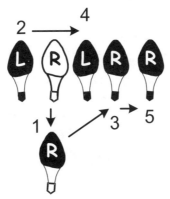

Woman's part 1 WCS Basic

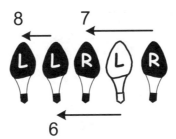

Woman's part 2 WCS Basic

The woman starts the WCS Basic step with her weight on her left foot and her right foot free. She takes a rock step back, then replaces her weight on her left foot. Then she takes a triple step to her right: step to the right with the right foot, step to the right with her left foot, step to the right with her right foot. Count the steps as: One, Two, Three And Four.

The second half of the WCS Basic has the woman taking a step to the left with her left foot on beat 5, then a step to the left with her right foot between beats 5 and 6, and then a step to the left with her left right on beat 6. Count the steps as: Five And Six.

WCS Under Arm Pass (Lady's turn)

The Under Arm Pass with Lady's Turn is a fun step that looks good and is easy to do. The man and woman start in the half open position with the man holding the woman's right hand in his left hand. After rocking back on the first beat, the couple then 'trade places' with the woman doing a counter-clockwise turn as she passes under the man's hand. The way the man leads this pattern is to draw the woman's right hand towards his right ear and then raise her hand up over the top of her head so she can

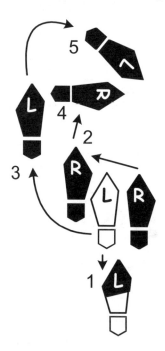

Man's part 1 WCS Under Arm Pass

turn underneath his hand. The woman should pass very close to the man as she turns. The man turns his body to face the woman at all times while she passes under his arm. At the end of the step both partners are facing each other, and the woman is at the opposite end of the 'Slot' from where she started.

For the man's part 1 the man rocks back on his left foot on beat 1. On beat 2, he takes a step forward and to his left with his right foot, crossing in front of his left foot. This gets the man's body out of the way of the woman who will be passing close by on his right. At the same time the man is taking his second step he leads the woman into the under arm turn by gently pulling her right hand towards his right ear. As she steps forward following the lead, the man raises her hand up over her head (about 2-3 inches above her head) and indicates a counter-clockwise turn by drawing his had toward himself and then out away from his body so the woman begins to turn facing away from the man rather than turning in to face him. Steps 3,4 and 5 are a triple-step for the man and he uses this triple-step to rotate his body so that he is facing the woman as she passes by. Step 3 is forward and to the left with the left foot on beat 3. Step four is a forward step with the right foot rotating 90 degrees to the right in between beats 3 and 4. Step five is a step around to the left of the right foot on beat 4 and is rotated still more towards the right so the man faces the woman.

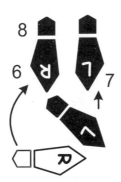

Man's part 2 WCS Under Arm Pass

The second part of the Under Arm Pass is the anchor step: the triple step that 'anchors' the pattern. The man takes a step back with his right foot on beat 5. The next step (seven) is taken in between beats 5 and 6 and brings the left foot next to the man's right foot so he is squarely facing the woman. Step 8 is

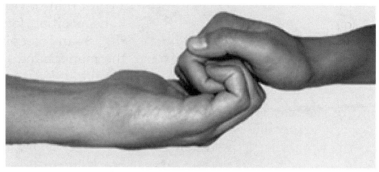

Hand Position Before Turn

Hand Position During Turn

Hand Position After Turn

www.DanceAce.com

essentially a step in place for the man with his right foot on beat 6.

Note: When leading the turn, it is important that the man not grip or squeeze the woman's hand. The hand position for swing dancing is like making a cup with the fingers and keeping the thumb out of the way. During the turn, the man's hand presses downward slightly on the palm of the woman's hand as she turns underneath. As in the illustrations, the couple's hands are like a 'ball and socket' when turning.

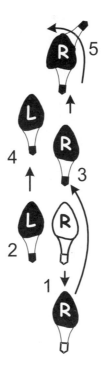

Woman's part 1 WCS Under Arm Pass

The woman begins this pattern by taking a rock step back on her right foot. On the second step, the woman takes a step forward on to her left foot. At this time she should feel the lead of the man drawing her hand forward and up. As the man leads the turn, the woman takes a step forward (step three) with her right foot on beat 3. This is the first step of a triple-step. Step four is taken forward with the left foot in between beats 3 and 4. Step five is the last step of the triple-step and is also the step where the woman pivots for a dramatic turn. (It is also possible to use the triple-step to turn more gradually) The woman can turn gradually or dramatically, but she should be done turning when she takes her fifth step on beat 4.

Tip: When a man raises a woman's hand up it almost always means the woman will be turning.

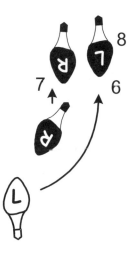

Woman's part 2 WCS Under Arm Pass

The second part of the Under Arm Pass is the anchor step. The woman takes a step back with her left foot on beat 5, the first step of a triple-step. Step seven is a step with the right foot to bring the feet together. Step 8 is a step in place with the left foot on beat 6.

WCS Left Side Pass

The side pass leads the woman down the 'slot' and lets her add a little flair to the turn at the end of the slot. The man steps back and to the side to let the woman run down the slot.

The couple can start in the open position, the half open, or even the closed position. The man takes a step backward and to the left with his left foot on beat one, turning his body ¼ turn to his left (counter-clockwise). As he does this, he pushes gently with his left hand to lead the lady to rock back as well. The next step is with the right foot slightly behind and to the right of where it was. This gets the man's body out of the woman's way so she can run down the

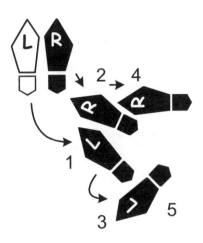

Man's part 1 Left Side Pass

slot. At the same time as the man is taking the first step, he must let go with his right hand if the couple started in the closed position.

The man leads the woman with his left hand down the slot which the woman uses to dance back and forth. Step three is a small step with the left foot on beat 3 and is the first step of a triple step that the man uses to turn his body to the left. Step four with the right foot is taken in between beats 3 and 4 and is a really just a change of weight. Step five takes a slight turn with the left foot on

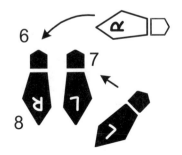

Man's part 2 Left Side Pass

beat 4. At this point the woman should be at the end of the slot and she will be turning so the man should keep his left arm firm for her turn.

For part 2 the next step is with the right foot on beat 5 and is the first step of a triple step. The man uses the first step to turn and face the woman who is now at the opposite end of the slot from where she started this pattern. The next step is with the left foot in between beats 5 and 6 and brings the left foot close in next to the right foot. The last step is with the right foot, in place, on beat 6.

Note: The final triple step in the WCSwing is almost always taken in place and is referred to as the 'anchor step' because it provides consistency and anchors the dance step.

TIP: Men, be aware of how much space you have on the dance floor and be careful not to lead your partner into another couple. Plan your dance patterns so you have space to execute the pattern without bumping into other couples. When you start the dance, make sure your 'slot' is clear.

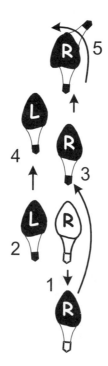

Woman's part 1 Left Side Pass

The woman begins this dance pattern with a rock step back on her right foot on beat 1. On beat 2 she replaces her weight on her left foot. On beat 3 she follows the man's lead to run down the slot and takes a step forward with her right foot. The next step is taken in between beats 3 and 4 and is a walking step forward with her left foot. The next step is a walking step with the right foot on beat 4 and is the final step of the first triple step. The diagram shows the woman's walking step to illustrate how the woman runs down the slot. Once she reaches the end of the slot, the woman pivots on her right foot to turn and face her partner.

Note: the woman has been walking in a straight line down the slot and should be at the end of the slot on beat 4 so she can make the turn (dramatic or smooth) at the end of the slot to face her partner again.

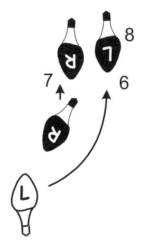

Woman's part 2 Left Side Pass

When the woman has reached the end of the slot, she pivots on her right foot to turn and face her partner. How she turns, and what flair or styling she chooses to add is up to her. This is an area where the woman can show off. After the 180 degree pivot on the right foot, the woman steps backward with the left foot (the first step of a triple-step) on beat 5, then steps with the right foot in between beats 5 and 6, and then steps in place with the left foot on beat 6. This second triple-step is called the 'anchor step'.

Putting it together

Swing dancing is great fun, and you can never do too many turns. Start off with the basic step and go to the under arm turn. Alternate between basic steps and turns, or you can lead two turns in a row. Then do a side pass and back to the basic. The side pass is especially nice if your partner is dizzy from all the turns. As always, mix and match the steps and you will build your confidence.

* * *

Rumba

The Rumba is the grandfather (grandmother?) Of the Latin dances, and is a blend of influences from Spain and Africa centered in Cuba. The Rumba gained popularity steadily through the Roaring Twenties, and was popular enough to be the title of a movie by 1935. Like the Tango today, the Rumba was seen as a sexy, cutting edge dance that spoke of a spontaneous lifestyle and represented more than just a dance.

The Rumba is a stylish, elegant spot dance in 4/4 time. Rumba music tends to be a little slower than the Cha-cha or the Salsa, and is the perfect dance for beginners. The Rumba uses the Latin Hip Motion for style and flair. Dancing the Rumba is fun and can be very sensual, almost like a Tango.

To get the Latin Hip Motion, which all the Latin dances feature, use your knees and feet to generate the motion rather than wagging your hips back and forth. With each step of the Rumba, the foot lands while the knee is bent. After the foot touches the floor, straighten the knee. As you prepare for the next step you must bend that knee. This is where the Latin Motion comes from: the leg you are standing on has a straight knee, the leg you are stepping with has a bent knee. This takes a little more effort than just walking, but it is one of the key differences between walking to music and dancing!

The Rumba also uses a modified closed dance frame called the Latin Frame. The dancers stand nose to nose and toes to toes, offset by about two inches to each person's left, as usual. The Latin Frame has the dancers a little closer together than the

Waltz or the Foxtrot, but farther away than when dancing the Tango. The man's left arm is held out in front rather than to the side, and his elbow is bent so that the man's forearm points straight up at the ceiling.

Style Points: Some instructors make a point of emphasizing how the Rumba box step starts on the Quick Quick rather than the Slow. That is a Fine Point to make. If you want to be proper, count off the first two beats and start the box with the "Side, Together" steps. Experiment to see which method works best for you. As your technique improves and you master the many elements of ballroom dancing, you can start the Rumba on the quick quick. To help beginners remember the steps better, it is illustrated the same as the other box steps: starting on the slow count.

Rumba Box Step

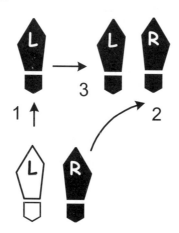

Man's part 1 Rumba Box Step

As always, the Man takes his first step with his left foot. Remember to flex the left knee and land the foot before straightening out the leg. This generates the Latin Motion. It is not necessary to bend the knee much at all to get the desired result. Feel free to overdo it at first to develop the habit, but relax and settle into a subtle Latin motion for the real dance. Step one is a (Slow: two beats) step forward. On step two the man's weight should be on his left leg (with knee straight) so the right foot is free to take a (Quick: one beat) step forward and slightly to the right. Keep the right knee flexed until the foot touches the floor. Step three is a (Quick) step to the right with the left foot to 'close' the feet back together.

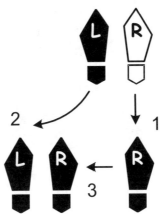

Man's part 2 Rumba Box Step

The second half of the Rumba Box begins with a (Slow) step backward onto the right foot. On Step two the man's weight should be on the right leg (with knee straight) so the left foot is free to take a (Quick) step backward and slightly to the left. Keep the left knee flexed until the foot touches the floor. Step three is a (Quick) step to the left with the right foot to 'close' the feet back to the starting position.

Tip: When the man takes a step backward, he should hold his right arm firm and gently 'pull' the lady. It is the job of the leader to communicate to his partner what he intends to do. If the man's right arm is limp it does not tell the woman anything.

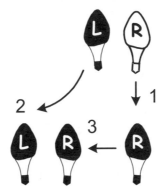

Woman's part 1 Rumba Box Step

The woman's first step is always with the right foot, and it is a (Slow: two beats) step backward, keeping the right knee bent until the foot touches the floor. On step two, the woman's weight should be on the right leg (with knee straight) so the left foot is free to take a (Quick: one beat) step to the left. The woman should keep pace with the man and take a big enough step. Step three is a (Quick) step to the left with the right foot to 'close' the feet back together.

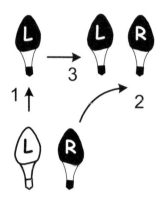

Woman's part 2 Rumba Box Step

The second half of the box is the woman's turn to step forward. The woman's left foot should be free with her weight on her right leg. The first step is a (Slow) step forward with the left foot. On step two the woman's weight should be on the left leg (with knee straight) so the right foot is free to take a (Quick) step forward and slightly to the woman's right. Keep the right knee flexed until the foot touches the floor. Step three is a (Quick) step to the right with the left foot to 'close' the feet back to the starting position.

The Box step provides a solid foundation to start from. Many Rumba patterns begin or end with a box step. For leaders it is also a great step to do while planning the next pattern or waiting for space to clear on the dance floor. It is also possible to use the Rumba box step like a forward alternate to move around the dance floor to a less crowded area.

Parallel Break

The Parallel Break gets its name from the parallel body position of the dancers during the 'break' part of the pattern. The break starts at the 'top' of the box step, so the man must lead the first half of a box step to prepare for the Parallel Break.

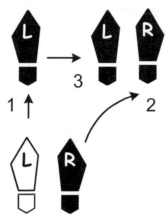

Man's part 1 Parallel Break

The man starts with a (Slow) step forward with his left foot, then a (Quick) step to the right side with his right foot, and then a (Quick) step to the right with his left foot to close. Now he is at the 'top' of the box.

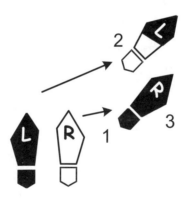

Man's par 2 Parallel Break

The next step for the man is a (Slow) step to the right with the right foot rotating his body clockwise 45 degrees. The man holds his left arm and right hand to rotate the woman 45 degrees into position for her parallel step. This prepares the dancers for the diagonal step that comes next. The second step has the man taking a (Quick) rock step forward and to his right with his left foot, around the outside of the woman's left foot. The third step is a (Quick) rock-replace back onto the man's right foot. The couple should be rocking in parallel for this part of the pattern.

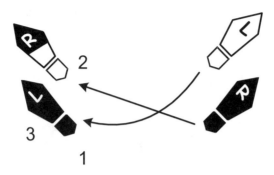

Man's part 3 Parallel Break

The third part of the Parallel Break has the man taking a (Slow) step with his left foot out to the left as he rotates 90 degrees counter-clockwise. The man also be rotating the woman in his arms as he turns so that she will be ready to take a step backward for her parallel step. Next the man takes a (Quick) rock-step forward onto his right foot, outside the woman's right foot. After rocking forward onto his right foot, the man then rocks back (Quick) onto his left foot.

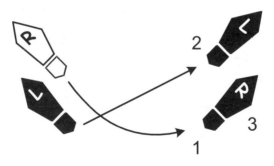

Man's part 4 Parallel Break

The fourth part of the Parallel Break is essentially a repeat of the second part with the man taking a (Slow) step to the right with his right foot as he rotates his body clockwise 90 degrees, using his arms to rotate the woman into position for her parallel step. Next he takes a (Quick) rocking step forward and to the right with his left foot, and a (Quick) step back replacing his weight onto the right foot.

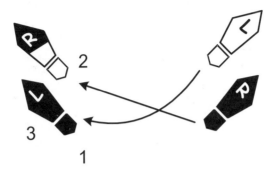

Man's part 5 Parallel Break

The fifth part of the Parallel Break is a repeat of the third part, and has the man taking a (Slow) step with his left foot to the left again. As before, the man will rotate counter-clockwise 90 degrees. The man will then take a (Quick) rock-step forward onto his right foot while using his arms to rotate the woman into position for her parallel step. After rocking forward onto the right foot, the man then (Quick) rocks back and replaces his weight onto his left foot.

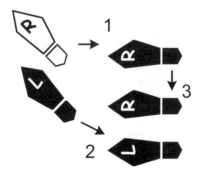

Man's part 6 Parallel Break

The 'exit' from the Parallel Break back to the box step is easy to lead. The man takes a (Slow) step backward with his right foot, then a (Quick) step to the side with his left foot, and a (Quick) closing step with his right foot. This should sound very similar to the back half of a box step, because it is the back half of a box step. To exit the Parallel Break, the man leads a 'back' box.

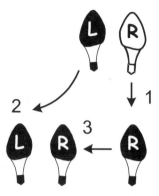

Woman's part 1 Parallel Break

The woman follows the man through the first half of the box step by taking a (Slow) step back with her right foot, then a (Quick) step to her left with her left foot, closing the feet with a (Quick) step to her left with the right foot.

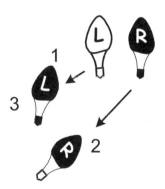

Woman's part 2 Parallel Break

The woman takes a (Slow) side step to the left with her left foot and rotates her body clockwise slightly so that she may take a step backward in parallel with the man's step forward. The man should lead this rotation with his right hand on the woman's shoulder blade. The next step is a (Quick) rock-step back with the right foot. Then a (Quick) step forward replacing her weight onto the left foot.

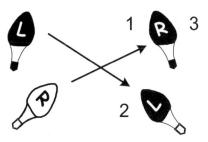

Woman's part 3 Parallel Break

The third part of the Parallel Break has the woman taking a (Slow) step right and forward with her right foot as she pivots counter-clockwise one quarter turn (90 degrees). The man will be leading this rotation with his upper body movements and with his right hand on the woman's shoulder blade. After she pivots, the woman takes a (Quick) rock-step back on her left foot, and then a (Quick) step forward replaces her weight back onto the right foot.

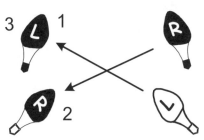

Woman's part 4 Parallel Break

Part four has the woman taking a (Slow) step left and forward with her left foot and rotating clockwise one quarter turn. The next step is a rock-step back with the right foot (Quick) and then a step forward replacing her weight on the left foot (Quick).

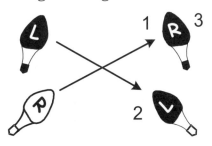

Woman's part 5 Parallel Break

Part five is a repeat of part three: (Slow) step right and forward with the right foot rotating counter-clockwise one quarter turn, (Quick) rock-step back with the left foot, (Quick) replace weight on the right foot.

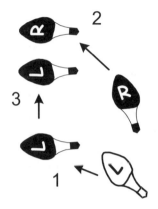

Woman's part 6 Parallel Break

It is possible that the man may continue the parallel break for a little longer, but when he wants to 'exit' the parallel break he may do it by leading the back half of a box step. For the woman this means a (Slow) step left and forward with the left foot, then a (Quick) step to the side with the right foot and a closing (Quick) step with the left foot.

Fall Away Break

The Fall Away Break gets its name by the way the couple seems to 'Fall' away from each other as they release from the closed position dance frame. The man lets go with his left hand and steps back and away while the woman lets go with her right hand and steps back and away. The couple maintains contact by the man's right hand on the woman's waist. The couple alternates falling away to one side and then the other. This is a simple pattern that can lead to many other patterns and is a good one for beginners to learn.

The man starts with a (Slow) step forward with his left foot, then a (Quick) step to the right side with his right foot, and then a (Quick) step to the right with his left foot to close.

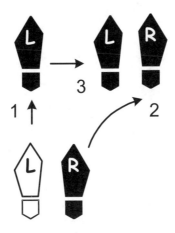

Man's part 1 Fall Away Break

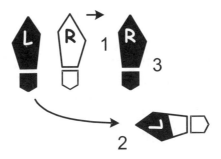

Man's part 2 Fall Away Break

Next the man takes a (Slow) step to the right with his right foot and releases the woman's right hand from his left with a slight push to let her know that she should 'fall away'. The man then takes a (Quick) rock-step back and to the left rotating his body counter-clockwise. (This is known as the 5th position in dance terminology, and this pattern can also be called the 5th position break) While the man steps back, he lowers his right hand from the woman's shoulder blade to her waist. The man then replaces his weight onto his right foot (Quick) and rotates clockwise to face the woman. While he is doing this he guides the woman to face him and prepares to release his right hand and 'catch' her with his left hand.

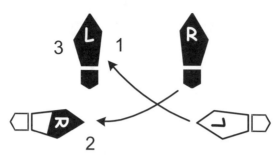

Man's part 3 Fall Away Break

The third part of the Fall Away Break is a mirror image of second part. The man takes a (Slow) step to the left with his left foot and releases the woman with his right hand and 'catches' her with his left hand on her waist. Because the man does not resume the closed position dance frame, the woman knows that she will be 'falling away' again.

The man then takes a (Quick) rock-step back to the right (5th position) with his right foot while he rotates his body clockwise. The man should have his left hand on the woman's waist. The man then replaces his weight onto his left foot (Quick) and rotates back to face the woman. While he is doing this he guides the woman to face him and prepares to release his left hand and 'catch' her with his right hand.

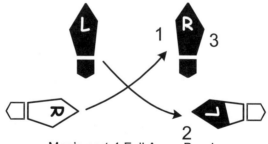

Man's part 4 Fall Away Break

Part four is a repeat of part two: the man takes a (Slow) step to the right with his right foot and releases the woman's right hand from his left with a slight push to let her know that she should 'fall away'. Then he takes a (Quick) rock-step back and to the left rotating his body counter-clockwise, catching the woman by the waist with his right hand. The man then replaces his weight onto his right foot (Quick) and rotates clockwise to face the woman.

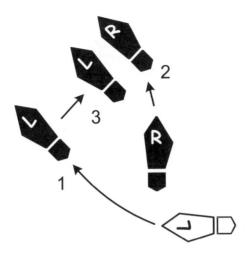

Man's part 5 Fall Away Break Exit to forward box

The 'falling away' steps may be repeated as many times as the man wishes. When the man is ready to end, or 'exit' the pattern, he will lead out of it from his right to his left. Specifically, after rocking back on his left foot, the man will lead a forward half box. To resume the closed dance frame position, the man raises his left hand so the woman knows to resume the dance frame. The woman will give him her right hand and then the man takes a (Slow) step forward with his left foot into a forward box step. This is followed by a (Quick) step to the side with his right foot and a (Quick) step to the side with is left foot to close.

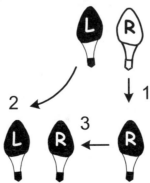

Woman's part 1 Fall Away Break

www.DanceAce.com

The woman follows the man through the back half of the box by taking a (Slow) step back with her right foot, then a (Quick) step to her left with her left foot, closing the feet with a (Quick) step to her left with the right foot.

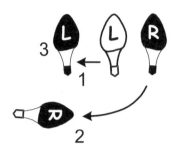

Woman's part 2 Fall Away Break

The Fall Away Break begins at the 'top' of the box step. The woman takes a (Slow) step to the left with her left foot. As she does this, the man will gently push off with his left hand releasing her right hand. This is the signal that the woman should 'fall away'. Falling away is a graceful (Quick) rock-step back and to the right with the right foot as the woman rotates one quarter turn clockwise. (This is known as the 5th position in ballet) Then the woman replaces her weight on her left foot (Quick) and turns counter-clockwise to face the man.

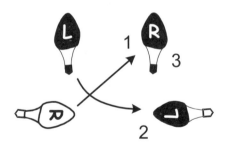

Woman's part 3 Fall Away Break

The third part is a mirror image of the second part. The woman takes a (Slow) step to the right with her right foot. As she does this, the man releases his right hand from her waist and catches her with is left hand on her waist. The woman then takes a (Quick) rock-step back and to the left with her left foot and rotates one quarter turn counter-clockwise. Then the woman replaces her weight on her right foot (Quick) and turns to face the man.

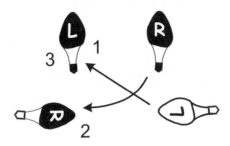

Woman's part 4 Fall Away Break

Part four is a repeat of part two. The woman takes a (Slow) step to the left with her left foot. As she does this, the man will gently push off with his left hand releasing her right hand. Then the woman takes a (Quick) rock-step back and to the right with the right foot as she rotates one quarter turn clockwise. Then the woman replaces her weight on her left foot (Quick) and turns counter-clockwise to face the man.

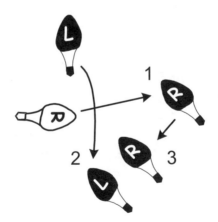

Woman's part 5 Fall Away Break Exit to forward box

When the man is ready to end, or 'exit' the pattern, he will hold up his left hand. This is the signal that the woman should give him her right hand and be ready to do something other than another fall away. The man might lead a turn, or a box step, or who knows what, so be ready to follow anything. In this case, the man is leading a forward box, so the woman will take a (Slow) step to her right and forward with her right foot. The couple will resume the closed dance frame position and the woman will take a (Quick) step back and to the left with her left foot, and then a (Quick) step to the side with her right foot to close.

Rumba Lady's Under Arm Turn

This pattern is simple and elegant, and may be used almost anywhere the man wants to liven things up. This step can be led from any other pattern where the man has his left foot free. This means that the Under Arm Turn can be used to exit the Fall Away Break, or after a box step, or immediately after exiting the Parallel break. The man simply takes a side step to his left and raises the woman's right hand. This is her cue to turn. After the turn, the man must use a 5th position break (without releasing the woman's right hand) to stay on the beat and lead into another pattern.

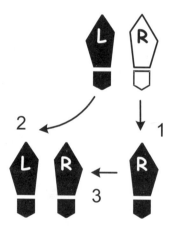

Man's part 1 Lady's Under Arm Turn

The footprint diagram shows the man finishing a box step to illustrate a typical 'starting' position. (Slow) Back (Quick) Side (Quick) Together.

For part 2 the man takes a (Slow) step to the left as he releases his right hand and raises the woman's right hand three to six inches above her head. To make sure she turns clockwise, the man should use a slight 'forward-back' circular motion with his

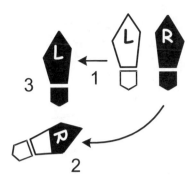

Man's part 2 Lady's Under Arm Turn

left hand. As the woman is turning, the man (Quick) rocks back on his right foot in the 5th position. The man should keep his right arm by his side with the elbow bent slightly and the hand relaxed. As the woman turns, the man replaces his weight (Quick) on his left foot and turns to face the woman.

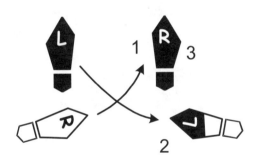

Man's part 3 Lady's Under Arm Turn

As the woman completes her turn, the man resumes the closed dance frame position and takes a (Slow) step to the right side with his right foot. Without letting go of her right hand (The woman's right hand should be in the man's left hand) the man takes a (Quick) rock-step back and to the left with his left foot in the 5th position. The man guides the woman to do the same by pushing slightly with his left hand while rotating the woman with his right hand on her shoulder blade. The man then (Quick) replaces his weight on his right foot.

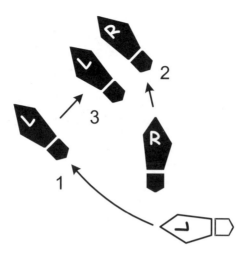

Man's part 4 Lady's Under Arm Turn

The man then takes a (Slow) step forward with his left foot to lead a forward half box step. Then he takes a (Quick) side step with his right foot and (Quick) closes with his left foot and he may finish the box step pattern or lead one of the break patterns above.

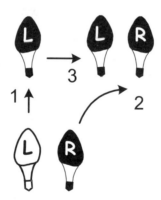

Woman's part 1 Lady's Under Arm Turn

The Lady's Under Arm Turn can be led from many steps. The diagram shows the woman finishing a box step to illustrate a typical starting position. (Slow) Forward (Quick) Side (Quick) Together.

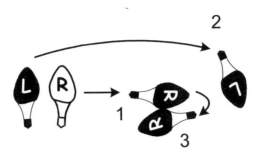

Woman's part 2 Lady's Under Arm Turn

The man will raise the woman's right hand up to indicate the woman will be turning as she takes her first step, which is a (Slow) step to the right with her right foot that lets the woman turn her body clockwise one quarter turn. The next step is a (Quick) step forward in the direction the woman is now facing with the left foot. The woman's weight should be on the left foot at this point, but her center-of-gravity should still be over her right foot. The next (Quick) step is not so much a step as a pivot of both feet with a weight change to the right foot. The woman does an 'about face' turning 180 degrees.

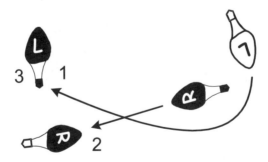

Woman's part 3 Lady's Under Arm Turn

After the pivot turn, the woman takes a (Slow) step forward and to the woman's right with her left foot as she turns clockwise to face the man. The man will resume the closed dance frame position as she does this. The next step is a (Quick) rock-step back with the right foot to the 5th position. The woman then takes a (Quick) step replacing her weight on her left foot.

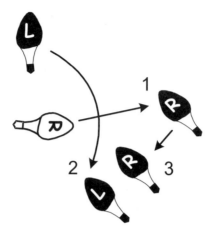

Woman's part 4 Lady's Under Arm Turn

To end the pattern and return to the box step the woman takes a (Slow) step forward and to the right with her right foot and rotates counter-clockwise to face the man. The woman then takes a (Quick) step backward with her left foot, and then a (Quick) closing step with her right foot.

Putting it together

Now you have several patterns to dance the rumba. To combine them into a dance is the man's job. Try starting with the box step, and when that is comfortable, lead into a parallel break. Then a box step and a Fall Away Break. After that another box and then a Lady's under arm turn. Use the left turning box (The Rumba can borrow from the Waltz here!) to change the view for the lady and do the steps again. It is also possible to lead the Fall Away Break directly into the Lady's Under Arm Turn. Or try leading the parallel break directly into the Lady's Under Arm Turn. As you become more comfortable with each step, you will develop the confidence to mix and match them in any combination depending on the music and your mood.

* * *

Cha-cha

The Cha-cha is a more recent dance that grew out of a dance called the Mambo. The Mambo resulted from the combination of American Jazz with the Rumba. In Cuba, the Mambo was danced occasionally with a triple step that was commonly referred to as the cha cha cha step. With a group of adoring fans, the 'Triple Mambo' also known as the 'Mambo Cha Cha Cha' developed into its own dance in the 1950s and the name was shortened to Cha-cha. The Cha-cha has a strong Latin flavor, and is in many ways like a Rumba in high gear.

The Cha-cha is a spot dance, and the music has four beats per measure. It can be fast, so the Latin Hip movement can get pretty wild. The Cha-cha uses the Latin Frame, and the woman is free to enhance the turns and breaks with dramatic gestures like in the Tango.

Basic Cha-cha

The Cha-cha triple step, or 'cha cha cha' of the music gives the dance it's name and timing. Some Cha-cha music has a heavy accent on the triple step that can not be missed. Cha-cha patterns are commonly counted 2, 3, 4 AND 1 where the 4-AND-1 falls on the cha cha cha. Getting started on the right beat is simply a matter of catching the last cha. Listen for... Cha cha cha then start counting after the third 'cha' with 2, 3, 4-AND-1. 2, 3, 4-AND-1, step, step, tri-ple-step - step, step, tri-ple-step.

For the basic step, the man takes a step to his left with his left foot on beat one, then a rock step backward with his right foot on beat two. On beat three he replaces his weight on his left foot, and then he does a triple step to his right starting on beat four with a step to the right with his right foot, followed by a step to the right with his left foot in between beats 4 and 1.

The second half is a step to the right with the right foot (to finish the triple) and then a rock step forward with the left foot. This is followed by a rock-replace step with the right foot and then a cha cha cha to his right. Then the pattern repeats itself.

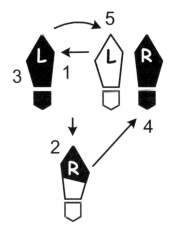

Man's part 1 Cha-cha Basic

The couple starts in the closed position, using the Latin Frame. The man's first step is to the left side with his left foot on beat 1 (beat one is the third 'Cha'). The man then rock-steps back on his right foot on beat 2 and replaces his weight on his left foot on beat 3. The next step is the first of the triple step, and has the man taking a step to his right with his right foot on the first 'cha', beat 4. The second step of the triple step is taken between beats 4 and 1, with the left foot stepping left to close the feet together.

Editor's note: Step 5 is a weighted step. The diagram shows an unweighted left foot to illustrate the starting position of the left foot, which happens to be exactly where the foot lands on step 5.

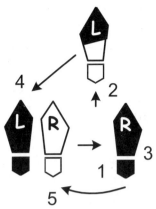

Man's part 2 Cha-cha Basic

The second part is very similar to the first part except the man rocks forward instead of backward. The man's first step is to his right with the right foot on beat 1 (this completes the triple step he started in the first part). The man then rock-steps forward on his left foot on beat 2 and replaces his weight on his right foot on beat 3. Then it is time for the 'cha cha cha' triple again, so the man takes a step to his left with his left foot on beat 4, and a step to the left with the right foot between beats 4 and 1 for the second 'cha'. With all this fancy footwork, it is good news that the dance frame is constant, with no upper body action to distract the dancers. This allows the dancers to concentrate on their feet.

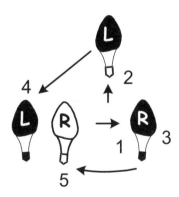

Woman's part 1 Cha-cha Basic

The woman's first step is to her right with the right foot on beat 1. The woman then rock-steps forward on her left foot on beat 2. The next step, on beat 3, has the woman replacing her weight back on her right foot. The lady then takes a step to her left with her left foot for the first 'cha' of the triple step. The last step is a step to the left with the right foot between beats 4 and 1 for the second 'cha' of the triple step.

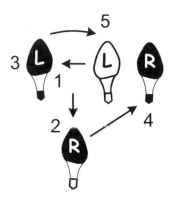

Woman's part 2 Cha-cha Basic

The woman's next step is to the left with the left foot on beat 1 for the third 'cha' which completes the triple step. The woman then rock-steps back on her right foot on beat 2, and replaces her weight on her left foot on beat 3. Then it is time for the 'cha cha cha' triple again, so the woman takes a step to the right with her right foot on beat 4 for the first 'cha', and a step to the right with her left foot between beats 4 and 1 for the second 'cha'. It may seem confusing to have a triple step split between two halves of the dance pattern, but in practice, the 'cha cha cha' is the easiest part of the dance and binds the steps together well.

Parallel Break

The Parallel Break is performed in the closed position. The couple begins with a 'half' of a basic step and then the man rotates to his right while rotating the woman to his left. The result is that the couple's bodies are parallel and next to each other, dancing 'shoulder to shoulder' which is an alternate name for this pattern.

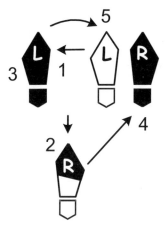

Man's part 1 Parallel Break

The first part is the same as the first half of the basic step. The couple remain in closed dance frame. Step left on beat 1, rock-step back on 2, replace on 3, step right with right foot on 4, close with left foot between beats 4 and 1.

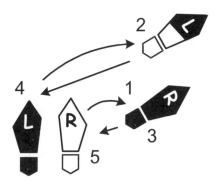

Man's part 2 Parallel Break

Now the man takes a step to his right with his right foot on beat 1, and guides the woman to rotate her body clockwise so she is looking over his left shoulder rather than his right shoulder. At the same time the man rotates clockwise slightly and takes a rock-step to his right and forward with his left foot, stepping behind and to the side of the woman's left foot on beat 2. The man then replaces his weight on his right foot on beat 3 and 'un-rotates' the woman as he steps to the left with his left foot on beat 4, the first 'cha'. Finally, the man steps to the left with his right foot to close his feet together between beats 4 and 1, the second 'cha'. At this point the couple should be in closed position facing each other.

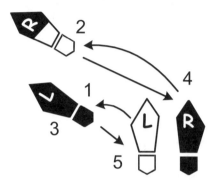

Man's part 3 Parallel Break

Next the man takes a step to his left with his left foot on beat 1, and guides the woman to rotate her body counter-clockwise so she is looking past his right shoulder. At the same time he rotates counter-clockwise slightly. Then he takes a rock-step to his left and forward with his right foot on beat 2, stepping behind and to the side of the woman's right foot. Then the man replaces his weight on his left foot on beat 3. Next hc 'un-rotates' the woman as he steps to his right with his right foot on beat 4, the first 'cha'. Finally, he steps to the right with his left foot to close his feet together between beats 4 and 1, the second 'cha'. Again, the couple should be in closed position facing each other.

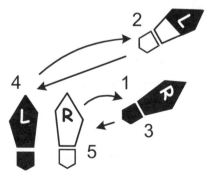

Man's part 4 Parallel Break

Part 4 repeats part 2: The man takes a step to his right with his right foot on beat 1, and rotates clockwise slightly to take a rock-step forward with his left foot on beat 2. The man then replaces his weight on his right foot on beat 3 and 'un-rotates' the woman as he steps to the left with his left foot on beat 4, the first 'cha'. Then the man steps to the left with his right foot to close his feet together between beats 4 and 1, the second 'cha'.

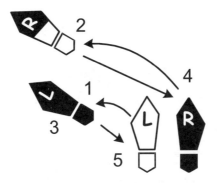

Man's part 5 Parallel Break

Part 5 repeats part 3: The man takes a step to his left with his left foot on beat 1, as he rotates counter-clockwise to take a rock-step forward with his right foot on beat 2. Then the man replaces his weight on his left foot on beat 3 and 'un-rotates' the woman as he steps to his right with his right foot on beat 4, the first 'cha'. Then the man steps to the right with his left foot to close his feet together between beats 4 and 1, the second 'cha'.

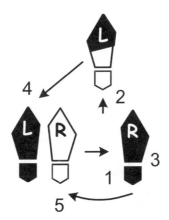

Man's part 6 Parallel Break

The man may continue to lead parallel breaks, other patterns, or he may choose to return to the basic step at this point. The 'exit' from the parallel break to the basic step is to lead a second half basic step pattern. The man takes a step to his right with the right foot on beat 1, then a rock-step forward on his left foot on beat 2. Because the man does not turn or rotate, the woman does not turn or rotate and it is clear that she should resume the basic step. Next, the man replaces his weight on his right foot on beat 3, and takes a step to the left with his left foot on beat 4 for the first 'cha'. The last step is a step to the left with the right foot between beats 4 and 1, the second 'cha', and he is ready for the next pattern.

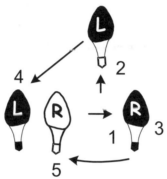

Woman's part 1 Parallel Break

The first part of the parallel break is the same as the first part of the basic step: The woman's first step is to the right with the right foot on beat 1. The woman then rock-steps forward on her left foot on beat 2. The next step has the woman replacing her weight back on her right foot on beat 3. The lady then takes a step to the left with her left foot on beat 4, the first 'cha'. Then the lady takes a step to the left with the right foot between beats 4 and 1 for the second 'cha'.

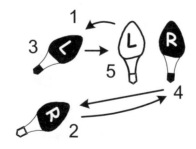

Woman's part 2 Parallel Break

The next step for the woman is a step to the left with her left foot on beat 1, where she will begin to rotate clockwise slightly as she rock-steps back with her right foot on beat 2. The man will guide her to rotate and look over his left shoulder as she does this. The next step is a rock-replace with her left foot on beat 3, followed by a step to the right with her right foot on beat 4 as she un-rotates back to face the man. Then she takes a step to the left with her left foot between beats 4 and 1 to close.

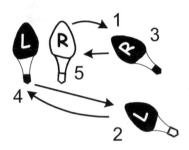

Woman's part 3 Parallel Break

Part three has the woman taking a step to the right with her right foot on beat 1. She will then rotate counter-clockwise slightly as she rock-steps back with her left foot on beat 2. The man will guide her rotation. The next step is a rock-replace with her right foot on beat 3, followed by a step to the left with her left foot on beat 4 as she un-rotates back to face the man. Then she takes a step to the right with her right foot between beats 4 and 1 to close.

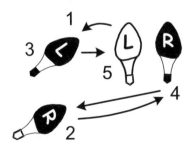

Woman's part 4 Parallel Break

Part 4 is a repeat of part 2: the woman steps to the left with her left foot on beat 1 and rotates clockwise as she rock-steps back with her right foot on beat 2. She replaces her weight on her foot on beat 3, and takes a step forward with her right foot on beat 4 to face the man. Then she takes a step to the left with her left foot between beats 4 and 1 to close her feet together.

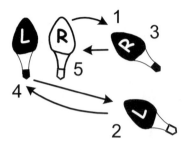

Woman's part 5 Parallel Break

Part 5 is a repeat of part 3: the woman takes a step to the right with her right foot on beat 1 and rotates counter-clockwise as she rock-steps back with her left foot on beat 2. Then she replaces her weight on her right foot on beat 3, and steps to the left with her left foot on beat 4 as she un-rotates back to face the man. Then she takes a step to the right with her right foot between beats 4 and 1 to close.

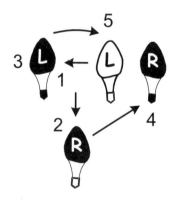

Woman's part 6 Parallel Break

When the man decides it is time to 'exit' the parallel break, he will simply lead another pattern, or resume leading the basic step. To resume the basic step from the parallel break part five, the woman will take a step to the left with her left foot on beat 1, then a rock-step back with her right foot on beat 2. She will then take a rock-replace step with her weight back onto her left foot on beat 3, and a step to the right with her right foot on beat 4. Finally, she will take a step to the right with her left foot between beats 4 and 1 to close.

New Yorker (Cross over break)

When comfortable with the basic step footwork, and the cha cha cha feels natural, it is time to try the New Yorker, which adds upper body motion to the dance. The couple changes from the closed dance frame to the half open dance frame in order to perform this pattern. To prepare for this pattern, the man leads his partner to release from the closed dance frame to the half open dance frame (holding one hand) while dancing the basic step. This may be done simply by the man releasing his right hand from the woman's left shoulder blade while dancing the basic step.

Once in the half open position, the man then rotates his body clockwise so that his left shoulder almost touches the woman's right shoulder. (The man rotating clockwise should rotate the woman counter-clockwise) This requires that the man hold his arms firm, and also requires that the woman hold her arms firm. If either dancer has limp arms, this pattern is very difficult to lead or follow. With firm arms, the man leads the rotation and the woman rotates to face the same direction as the man. The couple then repeat this move in the opposite direction, touching the

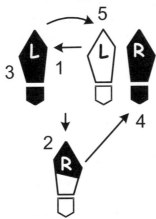

Man's part 1 New Yorker

man's right shoulder to the woman's left shoulder. Of course, this requires that the man release the woman's right hand while 'un-rotating' and take her left hand in his right hand to rotate (counter-clockwise) to face the opposite direction.

The first part of this pattern is identical to the basic Cha-cha step. The Man may choose to transition from the closed dance frame to the half open dance frame at this time, but the dancers must be in open dance frame or half open dance frame by the end of the first part of the New Yorker to execute the pattern. The man takes a step left with his left foot on beat 1, then a rock step back with the right foot on beat 2, replaces his weight onto his left foot on 3 and takes a step to the right with his right foot on 4 and a side step right with the left foot between beats 4 and 1.

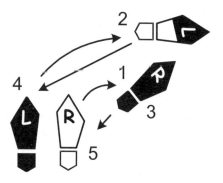

Man's part 2 New Yorker

Holding the woman's right hand in his left hand, the man takes a step to his right with his right foot and begins rotating his body 90 degrees (1/4 turn) clockwise to face the direction he is stepping. As he turns his body, he draws the woman's hand with him, rotating her body counter-clockwise to face the same direction (forward) as the man. The next step is a rock-step forward with the left foot on beat 2. The rotation is complete as the man takes the rock step. That is, he should be facing forward by the time he takes the rock step with his left foot. After the rock step, the man replaces his weight back onto his right foot on beat 3 and begins 'un-rotating'. He un-rotates (counter-clockwise) 90 degrees and takes a side step left with his left foot as he rotates back to face his partner on beat 4. The next step is a step left with the right foot to the close the feet together between beats 4 and 1.

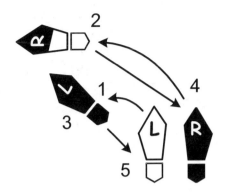

Man's part 3 New Yorker

For the next part, the man releases the woman's right hand with a gentle push away to let her know she should continue rotating clockwise, and takes her left hand in his right hand as it comes within reach. The man continues his own rotation counter-clockwise as he takes a step to his left on beat 1 with his left foot and turns his body to face the direction he is stepping. As he turns his body, he draws the woman's hand with him, turning her body to face the same direction (forward) as the man. The next step is a rock-step forward with the right foot on beat 2. Then a rock-replace step back onto the left foot on beat 3, and a step back and right onto the right foot on beat 4 as the man rotates clockwise to face his partner. The next step is a step left with the left foot to the close the feet together between beats 4 and 1.

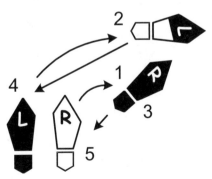

Man's part 4 New Yorker

Part four is the same as part two. The man releases the woman's left hand with a gentle push and takes her right hand with his left hand as he rotates clockwise and rotates the woman as he turns by holding her right hand in his left hand as he rocks forward.

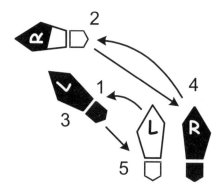

Man's part 5 New Yorker

Part five is the same as part three. The man rotates counter-clockwise to face left and rotates the woman as he turns by holding her left hand in his right hand as he rocks forward.

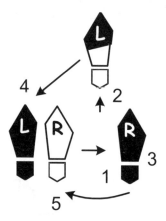

Man's part 6 New Yorker

It is possible to continue rotating left and then right as long as the man wishes to do so. When he is ready to return to the basic step, he keeps the woman's left hand with his right hand and leads a basic step. The man can also take the woman's right hand with his left hand to return to the open dance frame. The man's first step is to the right with the right foot on beat 1. The man then rock-steps forward on his left foot on beat 2. The man does not rotate, so the woman does not rotate. Because the woman is following the man, it is clear that she should resume the basic step. The man then replaces his weight on his right foot on beat 3 and takes a step to the left with his left foot on beat 4 for the first 'cha'. Then the man takes a step to the left with his right foot between beats 4 and 1 for the second 'cha', and he is ready to lead the next pattern.

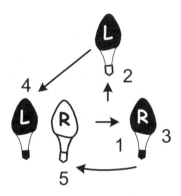

Woman's part 1 New Yorker

The woman's first step is to the right with the right foot on beat 1. The woman then rock-steps forward on her left foot on beat 2. The next step has the woman replacing her weight back on her right foot on beat 3. The lady then takes a step to the left with her left foot on beat 4, the first 'cha'. Then a step to the left with the right foot between beats 4 and 1 for the second 'cha'. The couple should be in the open or half open dance position at this point.

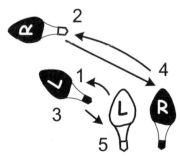

Woman's part 2 New Yorker

The man releases the woman's left hand and holds her right hand in his left hand. The man rotates the woman counter-clockwise to face forward as he takes his step. The woman takes a step to her left with her left foot on beat 1, and turns her body to face the direction she is stepping. She should end up facing the same direction (forward) as the man. The next step is a rock-step forward with her right foot on beat 2. Then she takes a step back onto the left foot on beat 3 as she 'un-rotates' clockwise to face her partner, and a side step to the right with her right foot on beat 4, the first 'cha'. The next step is a step with the left foot to the close the feet together between beats 4 and 1 for the second 'cha'.

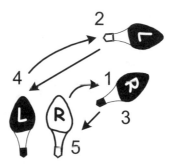

Woman's part 3 New Yorker

The man releases the woman's right hand with a gentle push and takes her left hand in his right hand. Then the woman follows the man by taking a step to her right with her right foot on beat 1 as she turns her body to face the direction she is stepping. As he rotates his body, he draws the woman's hand with him, rotating her body to face the same direction (forward) as the man. The next step is a rock-step forward with the left foot on beat 2. Then a step back onto the right foot on beat 3, and a step back onto the left foot on beat 4 as the couple rotates back to face each other. The next step is a step with the right foot to the close the feet together between beats 4 and 1.

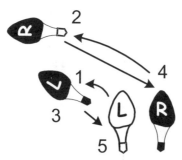

Woman's part 4 New Yorker

Part four is the same as part two, stepping to the left and rotating to face forward, then returning to face each other.

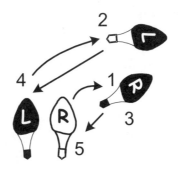

Woman's part 5 New Yorker

Part five is the same as part three, stepping to the right and rotating to face forward, then returning to face each other.

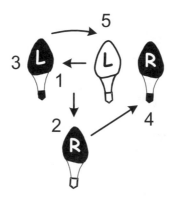

Woman's part 6 New Yorker

The woman's first step is to the left with the left foot on beat 1. The woman then rock-steps back on her right foot on beat 2. The next step has the woman replacing her weight on her left foot on beat 3. The lady then takes a step to the right with her right foot on beat 4, the first 'cha'. The last step is a step to the right with the left foot between beats 4 and 1 for the second 'cha'. The woman must be aware that the man may lead something other than the basic step, or may continue with the New Yorker for another turn or two. As a follower, the woman must not antici-pate what her partner will do and be ready for anything.

Cha-cha Lady's Under Arm Turn

The Lady's Under Arm Turn is always a good way to spice up a dance. The man has less complicated footwork to do than the lady, and can essentially continue with the basic step. The woman on the other hand has only to keep time with the music and turn when the man raises her hand above her head.

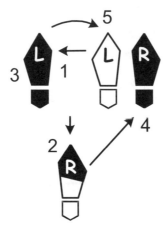

Man's part 1 Lady's Under Arm Turn

The first part of this step prepares for the actual turn. To do this, the man leads the first half of the basic Cha-cha step: step left with the left foot on beat 1, rock step back on the right foot on beat 2, replace weight on beat 3, step right with the right foot on 4 (Cha), step right with the left foot between 4 and 1 (Cha).

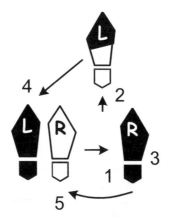

Man's part 2 Lady's Under Arm Turn

To prepare for the lady's under arm turn, the man continues the basic step footwork but releases his right hand from the woman's shoulder blade as he takes his rock step: step right with the right foot on beat 1, rock step forward on the left foot on beat 2 and drop the right hand from woman's shoulder blade. This frees the woman to turn, and also indicates to her that the man is preparing to lead something other than a basic step. Replace weight on the right foot on beat 3, step left with the left foot on beat 4 (Cha), and step left with the right foot between beats 4 and 1 (Cha).

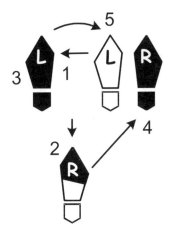

Man's part 3 Lady's Under Arm Turn

The man raises his left hand, and consequently the woman's hand, over her head as he takes a step to the left with his left foot on beat 1. When the man rocks back on his right foot on beat 2, the woman pivots on her right foot, turning clockwise under the man's arm. On beat 3 the man replaces his weight on his left foot and lowers his left hand. On beat 4 the man takes a step to his right with his right foot and resumes the Latin dance frame with the lady as they do the cha cha cha triple steps to the right. The next step for the man is a step right with the left foot between beats 4 and 1.

The last part of the pattern (below) is the second half of the basic step: step right with the right foot on beat 1, rock step forward on the left foot on beat 2, replace weight on beat

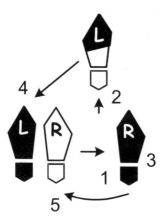

Man's part 4 Lady's Under Arm Turn

3, step left with the left foot on 4 (Cha), step left with the right foot between 4 and 1 (Cha).

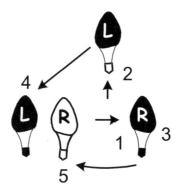

Woman's part 1 Lady's Under Arm Turn

The first part of this pattern prepares for the actual turn. To do this, the woman follows the first half of the basic Cha-cha step. The woman steps to her right with the right foot on beat 1, then rock-steps forward on her left foot on beat 2. Then replaces her weight back on her right foot on 3, followed by a step to her left with her left foot for the first 'cha' of the triple step. The last step is a step to the left with the right foot between beats 4 and 1 for the second 'cha' of the triple step.

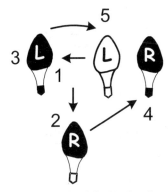

Woman's part 2 Lady's Under Arm Turn

The woman's next step is to the left with the left foot on beat 1 for the third 'cha' which completes the triple step, followed by a rock-step back on her right foot on beat 2. To prepare for the lady's under arm turn, the man releases his right hand from the woman's shoulder blade as she takes her rock step. This makes it possible for the woman to turn, and is also the indication that the man is preparing to lead something other than a basic step. The woman then takes a rock-replace step on 3, and a step to the right with her right foot on beat 4 for the first 'cha', and a step to the right with her left foot between beats 4 and 1 for the second 'cha'.

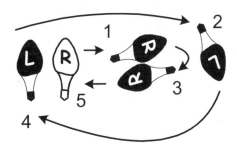

Woman's part 3 Lady's Under Arm Turn

The man will begin raising the woman's right hand as she takes a step right with her right foot. When the man's hand is above her head, the woman pivots on her right foot and takes a step with her left foot across her body to the right with her left foot on beat 2. This step turns the woman clockwise under the man's arm. The next step is a step with the right foot to complete the turn on beat 3, then a step with the left foot to the left on beat 4. At this point, the woman should be facing her partner again and be close enough to resume the Latin Dance Frame. The last step is a step to the left with the right foot between beats 4 and 1 to close the feet together.

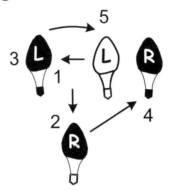

Woman's part 4 Lady's Under Arm Turn

After the turn is complete, the couple resume the Latin Dance Frame in closed position and complete the second half of the Cha-cha basic step: step left with the left foot on 1, rock-step back on her right foot on 2, rock-replace on 3, step to the right with the right foot on 4, and a step to the right with her left foot between beats 4 and 1 for the second 'cha'.

Putting it together

The Cha-cha is a lively Latin dance, and should be danced with that in mind. Start with the basic step and have fun with it. It is possible to dance the triple step forward and backward as well as side to side. When comfortable with the basic step, add the parallel break, then back to the basic step. When you are ready, add the New Yorker. When these steps flow, drop into the half open position and lead the Lady's Under Arm Turn. If you can lead the basic step to the New Yorker and then directly into the Lady's under arm turn, you have mastered the beginning steps of the Cha-cha.

* * *

Salsa

Salsa dancing covers a wide variety of styles and music. The dance itself may be a Spot dance, that is danced in one place or 'spot', or it may be danced as a traveling dance, moving about the dance floor to the Line of Dance. As one would imagine, with such a variety, there is no easy way to trace the roots of the dance. There is a large element of the Rumba, and some people say the Salsa evolved from the Mambo, much like the Cha-cha did. Salsa is usually danced to music of a medium to fast tempo, so the steps tend to be small fast.

The Latin motion that is the trademark of the Rumba is less emphatic in the Salsa. Just a little bit of hip motion is enough for the Salsa, because there is so much other motion to the dance. The relaxed way the dancers step is the key: relaxed, but not loose or sloppy.

The way steps are counted in the Salsa evolved from the Quick Quick Slow of the Rumba. The Salsa is a much faster dance than the Rumba, so a full two beat slow count is too slow. For many schools of dance, Salsa steps are counted 1, 2, 3 rest, 5, 6, 7, rest which results is something very close to quick quick slow, quick quick slow. The 'slow' step is not really a slow step, but there is a pause or a 'hold' on the third and seventh steps. Just like the Rumba and Cha-cha, the Salsa uses the Latin Dance Frame.

Salsa Basic

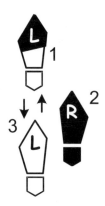

Man's part 1 Salsa Basic

The man takes a rock step forward with his left foot on the first beat and replaces his weight on his right foot immediately on the second beat. The man then takes a quick step back onto his left foot on the third beat and 'holds' for one beat.

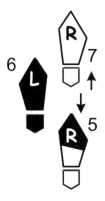

Man's part 2 Salsa Basic

The man takes a rock step back with his right foot on the fifth beat and immediately replaces his weight on his left foot on beat six. The man then takes a quick step forward onto the right foot on the seventh beat and 'holds' for one beat.

TIP: The fast music of the Salsa makes it very important to take small steps. It is also good to keep the feet close together, with the majority of weight on the balls of the feet.

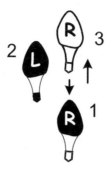

Woman's part 1 Salsa Basic

The woman takes a rock step back with her right foot on the first beat and immediately replaces her weight on her left foot on beat two. The woman then takes a quick step forward onto her right foot on the third beat and 'holds' for one beat.

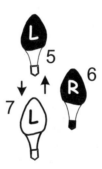

Woman's part 2 Salsa Basic

The woman takes a rock step forward with her left foot on the fifth beat and replaces her weight on her right foot immediately on the sixth beat. The woman then takes a quick step back onto her left foot on the seventh beat and 'holds' for one beat.

Salsa Side Basic

The Salsa side basic allows the dancers to execute a wide variety of patterns. As with any basic step, it is simple and lays the foundation for more complicated steps to be added in later.

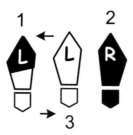

Man's part 1 Salsa Side Basic

The man takes a small, quick step to the left with his left foot on the first beat. The man only touches the ball of his foot to the floor and puts all his weight on the left foot without moving his body. The effect is very much like a rock-step to the side. The man then puts his weight back onto his right foot on the second beat; just like a rock replace step. On the third beat the man takes a step to the right with his left foot so that his feet are back to the same place he started. On the fourth beat the man 'holds', taking no step, with his weight is on his left leg.

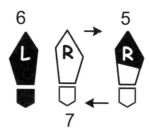

Man's part 2 Salsa Side Basic

The man takes a small, quick step to the right with his right foot on the fifth beat. As before, the man only touches the ball of his foot to the floor puts all his weight on the left foot like a rock-step to the side. The man then replaces his weight on his left foot on the sixth beat. On the seventh beat the man takes a step to the left with his right foot so that his feet are back to the same place he started. On the eighth beat the man 'holds', taking no step, with his weight on his right leg.

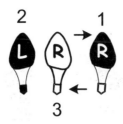

Woman's part 1 Salsa Side Basic

The woman takes a small, quick step to the right with her right foot on the first beat. She only touches the ball of her foot to the floor and puts all her weight on her left foot, just like a rock-step to the side. The woman then takes a step in place with her left foot on the second beat. On the third beat she takes a step to the left with her right foot so that her feet are back to the same place they started. On the fourth beat the woman 'holds', taking no step with her weight on her right leg.

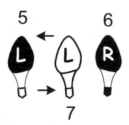

Woman's part 2 Salsa Side Basic

The woman takes a small, quick step to the left with her left foot on the fifth beat. As before, the woman only touches the ball of her foot to the floor and puts all her weight on the left foot. The woman then takes a step in place with her right foot on the sixth beat. On the seventh beat the woman takes a step to the right with her left foot, bringing her feet back to the same place she started. On the eighth beat the woman 'holds', taking no step, with her weight on her left leg.

Cross Body Lead

The Cross Body Lead allows the dancers to travel a bit and change the direction they are facing. This pattern is simple, but looks fancy, and is useful in preparing for another pattern that takes more space than is available in the current location.

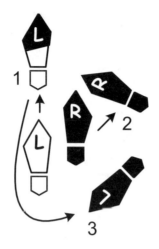

Man's part 1 Cross Body Lead

The couple start in the closed position. From the Salsa Basic step, the man takes a rock step forward with his left foot, but rather than replacing his weight on his right foot where it was, he takes a step to the side and rotates his body counter-clockwise a quarter turn (90 degrees) and lets go with his right hand. On the third beat he takes a step back and to his left so that he has stepped out of the way of the lady when she 'crosses' over. On the fourth beat the man 'holds' his feet in place as he leads the lady to step directly forward across his body by drawing his left hand across to his left side at waist level. It is important not to raise

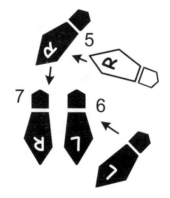

Man's part 2 Cross Body Lead

the hand up or the woman will turn the wrong way. In this pattern the woman does not turn under the arm, she turns like a whip.

For part 2 the man uses his left hand to lead the lady across, and as she takes her step forward on 5, he leads her in a 'fan' where she pivots dramatically (like a whip) on her left foot 180 degrees to face the man. As he leads the 'fan', the man takes a step forward and to his right with his right foot, rotating counter-clockwise to face the lady. On the sixth beat the man takes a step with his left foot to his right. On the seventh beat the couple is facing each other again as the man takes a step with his right foot to close his feet together. On the eighth beat the man 'holds' with his weight on his right leg.

Tip: The Cross Body Lead is a stylish way to change from the closed position to the half open position. The man can resume the closed position if he chooses, or lead another pattern from the half open position.

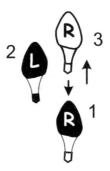

Woman's part 1 Cross Body Lead

The footwork for the first part of the Cross Body Lead is the same as the woman's basic step. The woman takes a rock step back with her right foot on the first beat and immediately replaces her weight on her left foot on beat two. At this point the man has stepped to the side and cleared a path for the women to step forward. The woman then takes a quick step forward onto her right foot on the third beat and continues forward, following the lead of the man. In this pattern the woman does not 'hold' on 4, she continues moving forward gracefully.

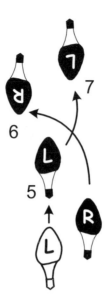

Woman's part 2 Cross Body Lead

On beat 5 the woman takes a step forward with her left foot and pivots counter-clockwise 180 degrees to face the man. This can be a dramatic pivot if the woman wishes, and is an opportunity for the woman to show her style. After the pivot the woman takes a step back with her right foot and then a step back with her left foot on beat seven and 'holds' for beat eight. At this point she should be facing her partner in the half open dance frame, or her partner may resume the closed Dance Frame.

Lady's Outside Turn

The Lady's Outside Turn has very similar footwork to a swing dance step, but the style and rhythm of the salsa makes this pattern look like a salsa dance step through and through.

From the half-open position, the man takes a quick step forward and out to the left with his left foot on beat one. On the second beat the man takes a step forward with his right foot and rotates his body (and right foot) clockwise towards the woman. As he does this, he draws the woman's right hand toward his right ear. Drawing (pulling) the woman's hand forward (from her perspective) and upward leads her to take a step forward and prepare for a turn. The man then takes a quick step with his left foot

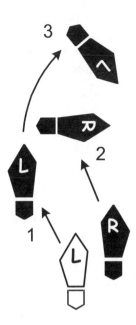

Man's part 1 Lady's Outside Turn

rotating his body clockwise so he faces toward the woman as she passes by. At this point the man leads the woman to turn by raising his hand up over her head. The man leads the woman to turn counter-clockwise and then 'holds' on beat four as she turns.

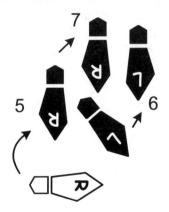

Man's part 2 Lady's Outside Turn

On beat five the man takes a step back with his right foot and rotates to face squarely toward his partner. He lowers his hand after the turn to the half-open dance frame position. Next he takes a step back with his left foot on beat six, and a step with his right foot to bring his feet together on seven and 'holds' on beat eight.

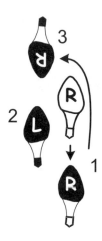

Woman's part 1 Lady's Outside Turn

The woman begins the Lady's Outside Turn with the basic step (rock-step) back with her right foot on beat one. The man will step to the side and lead the woman to take a step forward, so she replaces her weight on her left foot on beat two. The man will be raising her hand up over her head at this point, which indicates a turn. The woman then takes a step forward with her right foot and pivots counter-clockwise 180 degrees to face her partner. The woman has a little extra time to complete the turn because the man is 'holding' on beat four.

The woman then takes a step back with her left foot on beat five, and a rock-step back with her right foot on beat six. Beat seven has the woman replacing her weight on her left foot and 'holding' for beat eight.

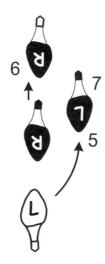

Woman's part 2 Lady's Outside Turn

Putting it together

Dancing the salsa is an expression of fun, passion, and style. Watch the other dancers on the floor to see how they embody the Salsa rhythm and flair. Start out with the basic step, and when you are comfortable with it, add a cross body lead. The cross body lead is good for changing the 'view' for yourself and your partner. The cross body lead also gives the lady a chance to add flair as she turns. It is possible to continue with the basic step or a turn, or even another cross body lead. Combining the steps in different order makes the dance more interesting, challenging, and fun. By mixing and matching the steps, it can look as if the dancers know more patterns! If the couple add the lady's outside turn after the cross body lead it looks like a much more complicated pattern. Often times dancers on the floor look most impressive when they perform simple patterns with confidence and enthusiasm. The fun they are having translates to their motions and the style of their dancing. Practice leads to confidence, and confidence is the key to success.

* * *

Next Steps

This book is an introduction to ballroom dancing, and as such it is just the tip of the iceberg. Several dozen patterns are presented here, but there are several dozen more patterns for each dance. Ace of Hearts Publishing has Intermediate level books containing many of these additional patterns. Visit the DanceAce website for previews and ordering information.

Dancing is a life long activity and can be enjoyed and improved upon endlessly. The most important next step is to go out and dance! Practice these patterns until they are second nature. When your body feels the music and flows through the step patterns, it is a true delight.

* * *